REFLECTIONS IN RHYME

KEVIN O'DOWD

New Haven Publishing Ltd

Published 2023
First Edition

New Haven Publishing Ltd
www.newhavenpublishingltd.com
newhavenpublishing@gmail.com

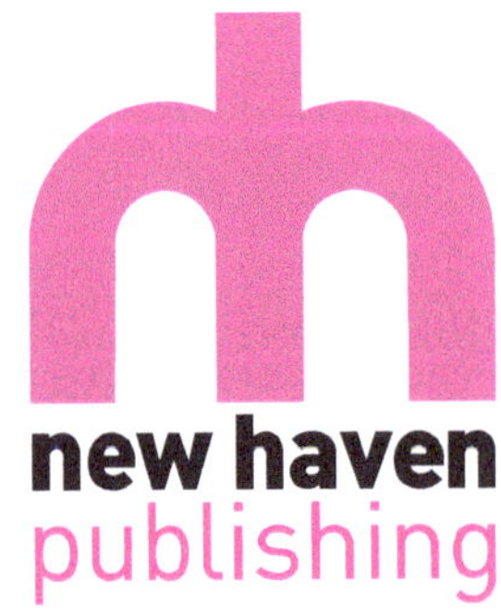

ISBN: 978-1-912587-83-4

FOREWORD

by **Boy George**

MY BROTHER KEVIN

My brother Kevin is loud
Stands out in and draws a crowd
Talks to everyone often shouts
Knows all about the world
And all it's ins and outs
He's stylish likes dancing
Turns up at every party
Is always the first to go home
Where he can write and be alone
He's creative, compulsive,good with his hands
Collects old junk like sideboards and prams
The floor is littered with his personality
My brother Kevin is dotty like me
A builder boss poet
What you get is what you see
My brother Kevin, an all encomposing entity

BOY GEORGE XXX

DEDICATION

To my
beautiful mother

MOTHER NATURE'S FURY

To the People of Turkey and Syria

Mother Nature crosses borders with impunity
She doesn't distinguish between the rich or the poor
Once she decides that she's going to vent her frustrations
she can create enough carnage and more devastation than any world war
Whereas a missile will take out a building or two at a time
Mother Nature can raise a whole city down to the ground
Whereas a couple of well aimed torpedoes take a battle ship down
Mother Nature's tsunami will create a wave
big enough for millions of people to drown
So messing with Mother Nature is never a good idea
She will pay us back for our arrogance more than ten fold
So we all need to remember the future belongs to our children
And we need to leave them a future behind when we eventually go

INDEX

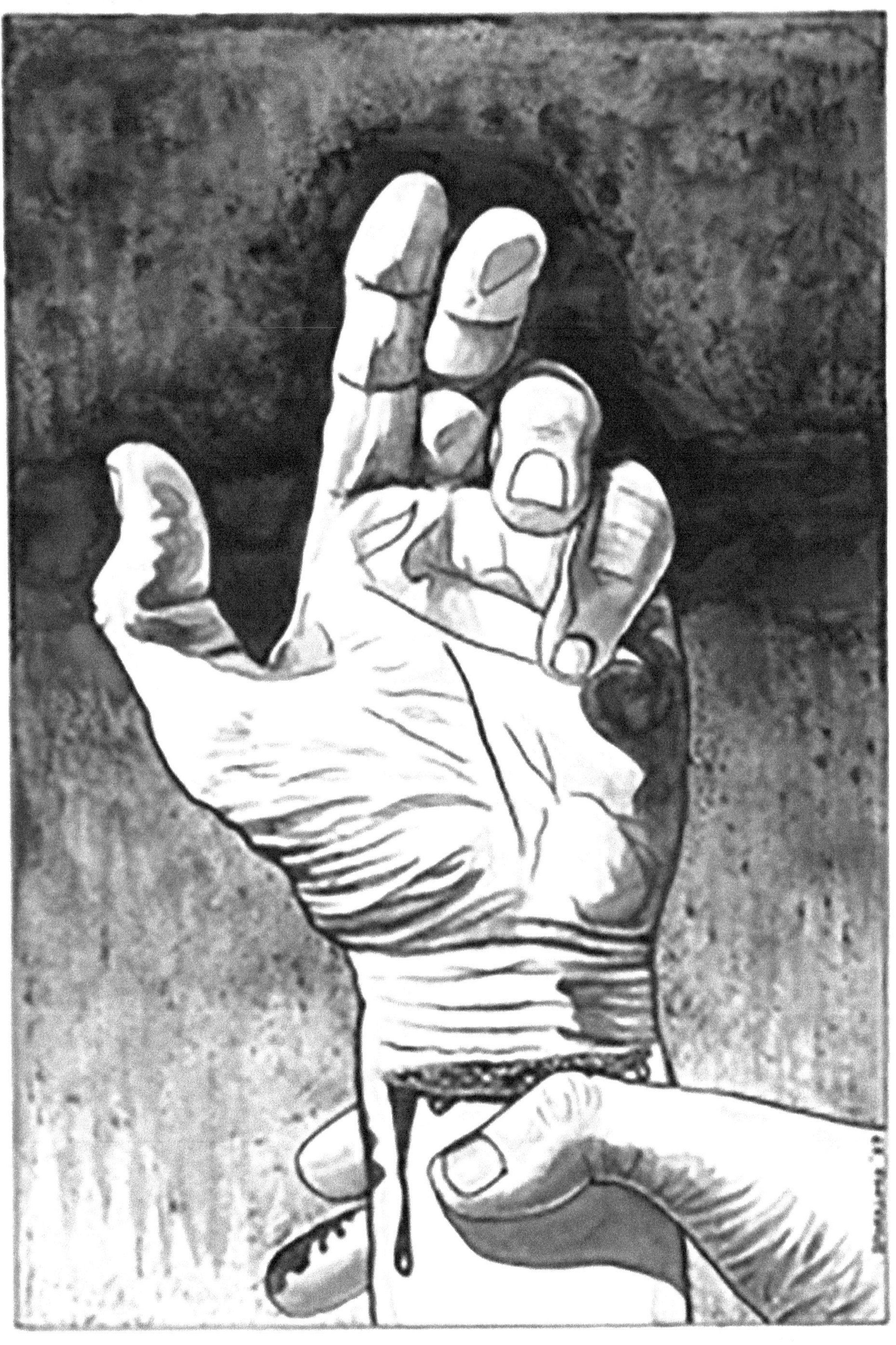

Illustration by Mark Campbell

TOO YOUNG AND TOO FOOLISH

Too young and too foolish
To learn from mistakes
Like walking on eggshells
Convinced they wouldn't break
Bending the rules
To suit my own needs
Cutting my skin
And then watching it bleed
Too young and too foolish
Much too thick skinned
Thinking I was entitled
Obviously destined to win
Of course I was special
That was easy to see
I just wanted it all
I'm quite easily pleased
I didn't need to queue up
Just open the door
I'll take that for now
But I deserved so much more
Too young and too foolish
To understand
That it wasn't as simple
As just having a plan
And when things went wrong
You obviously couldn't blame me
After all I was entitled
That was quite plain to see
But how can this happen
How could it be
Being forced to acknowledge
That it ain't all about me
I just couldn't believe
They could make such a mistake
I mean I was after all destined
To have the world on a plate
Too young and too foolish
Much too thick skinned
Thinking I was entitled
Obviously destined to win
Deserving forgiveness
For all of my sins

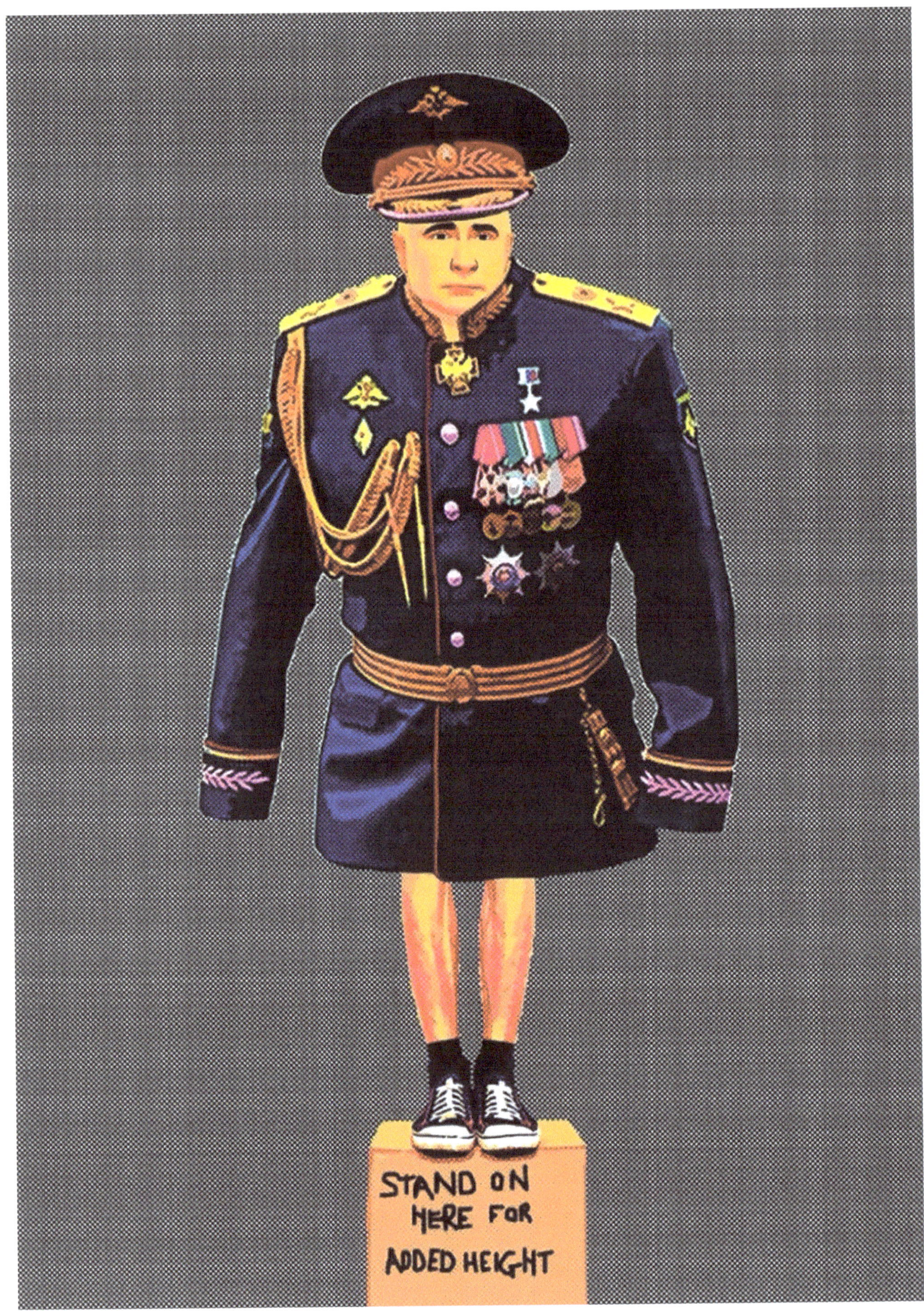

Illustration by Dean Stockley

UNDERSTANDING

They say that God forgives
No matter what you've done
So turn your back on violence and indifference
Put aside your bullets, bombs and guns
Reach out towards your neighbour
Sit down and break some bread
Celebrate the life you're living
Because you'll be a long time dead
We can't afford to let it be about religion
A man's colour, race or creed
His political persuasions or his sexuality
It ain't about the house you own
How much that car costs on your drive
It's all about compassion, love and above all understanding
The only way the human race is ever going to survive

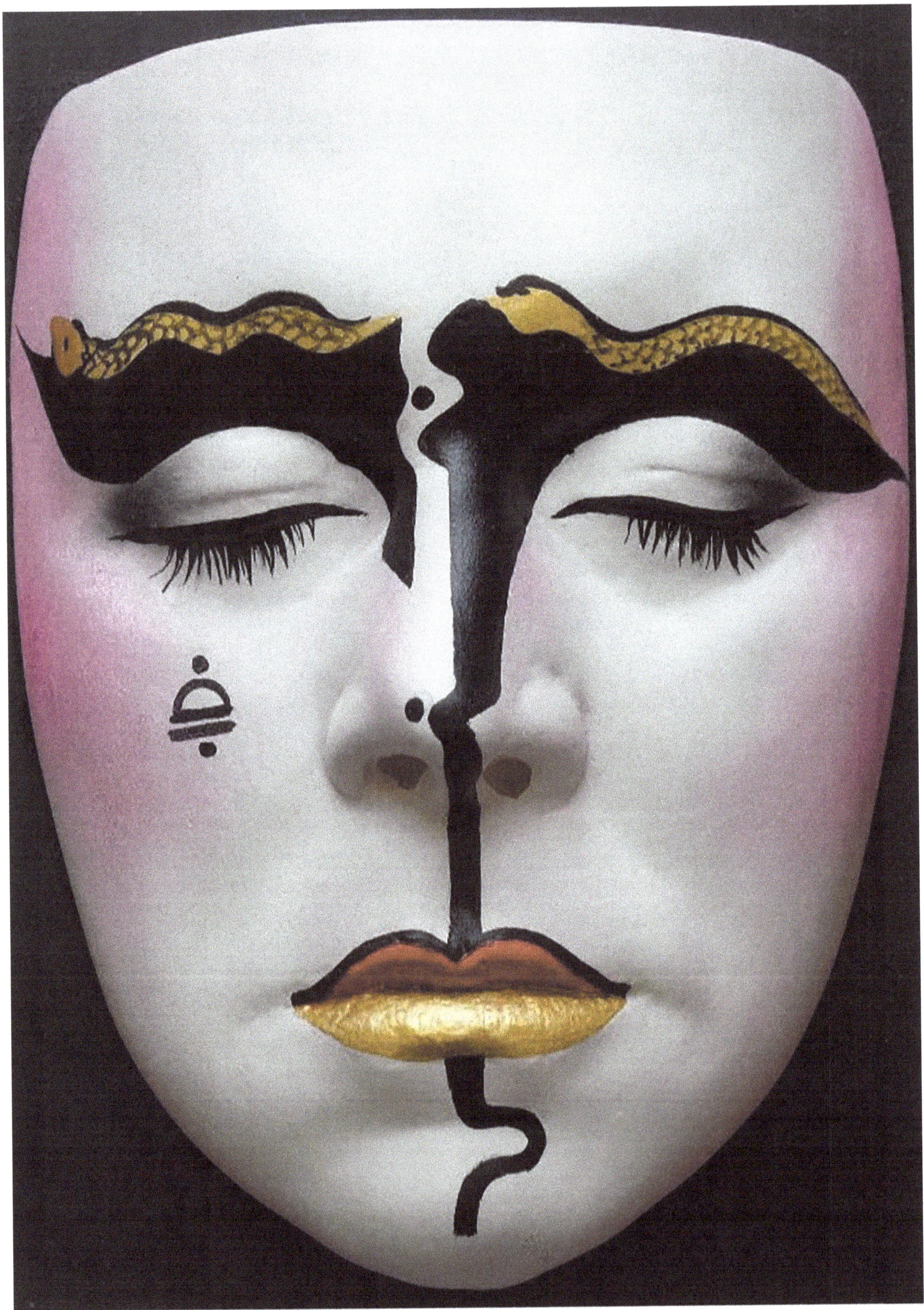

Illustration by Mark Wardel AKA TradeMark

COMING OF AGE

I was naked, afraid
Alone in the dark
The only sound I could hear
Was my own beating heart
I was lying here thinking
My life had to change
And the moment had come
For me to turn the next page
I was screaming in silence
I was falling apart
My breathing felt laboured
It was barely a gasp
And that was the moment
I decided to take off the mask
Life in the valleys
Was boring and grey
The people around me
Had nothing to say
I wanted a life
I needed the buzz
The nightclubs were calling
Come and join us
This was my moment
My coming of age
The time had now come
To turn the next page
It was all about fashion
About showing off
New Romantics and punks
Drag queens and goths
Boys wearing makeup
Girls dressed like men
The doors to the Blitz
Would open at ten
The Blitz was the place
Where dreams were explored
A boy from the valleys
Working the door
The launch pad for pop stars
The peacock brigade
Who transformed dressing up
Into artistic displays

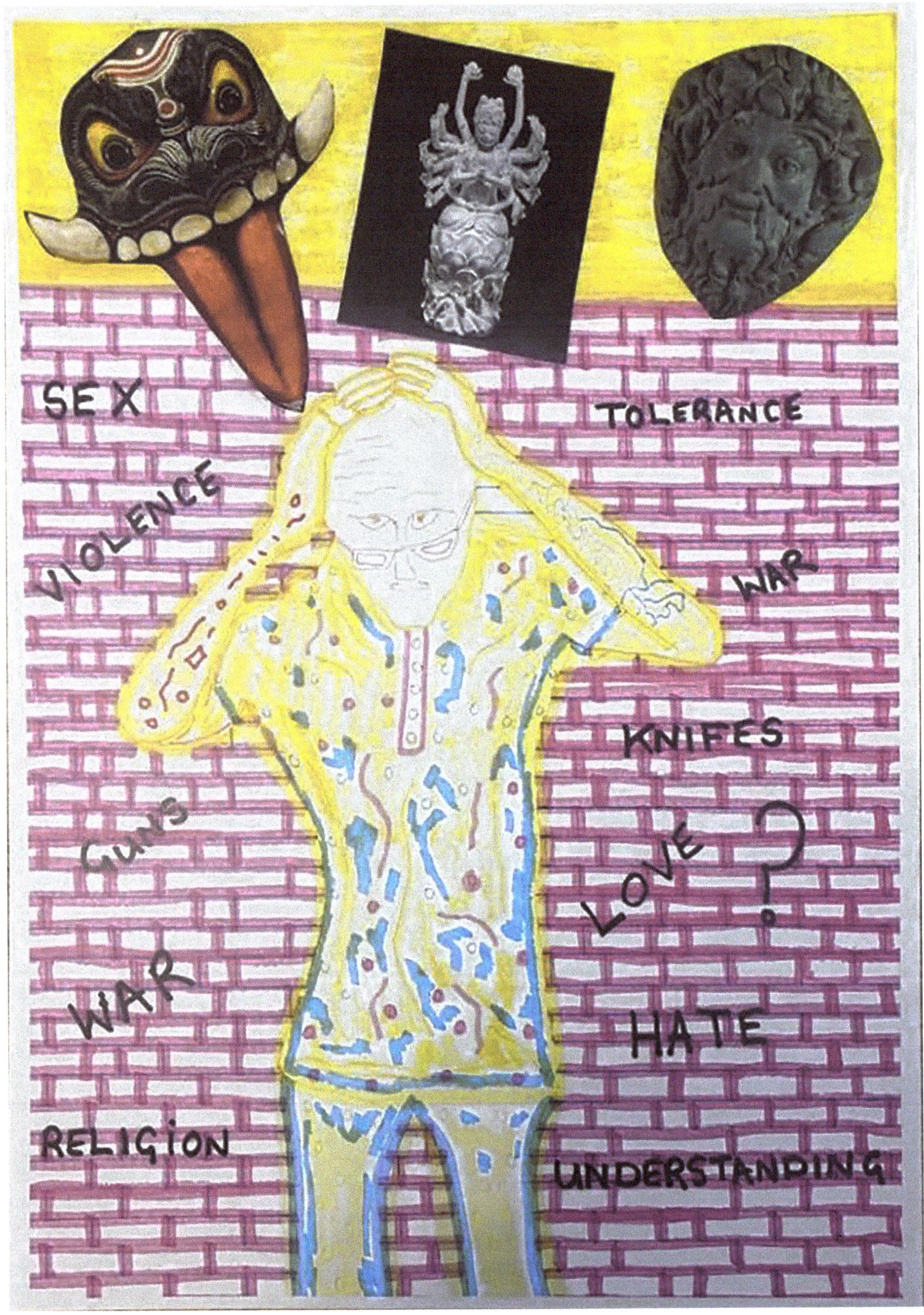

Illustration by Gerald O'Dowd

THE WORLD WE LIVE IN

We live in a world full of anger and hate
Jealousy, envy and greed
A world where children are dying
Every day from disease and starvation
Right under the noses
Of those who have much more than they need
We live in a world where weapons of war
Are actually valued above education
Where those we entrust to look after our interests
End up plundering the wealth of the nation
We live in world where one's choice of religion
Is now often a matter of life and death
Despite the fact that it's long been agreed
That there is but one god
Now we're slaughtering each other
In order to prove whose version of god is the best

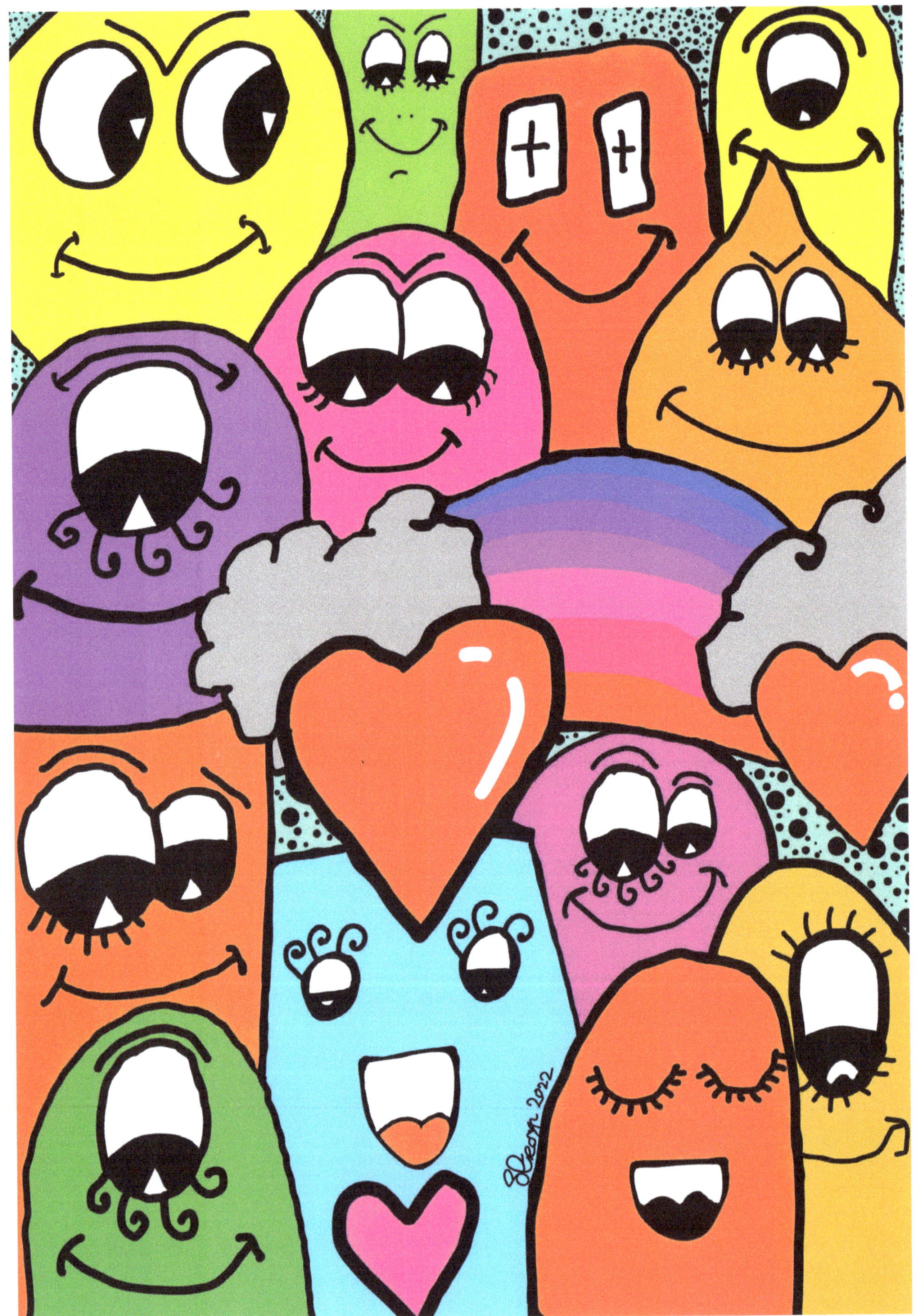

Illustration by Shaun George

WHAT

What is love
Without passion
A fire
Without flames
A question
That cannot be answered
Or a feeling
You just can't explain
The truth is
It really don't matter
Love's whatever
You want it to be
Like they say
You can't buy love
Or even rent it
So it's only real love
When it's free

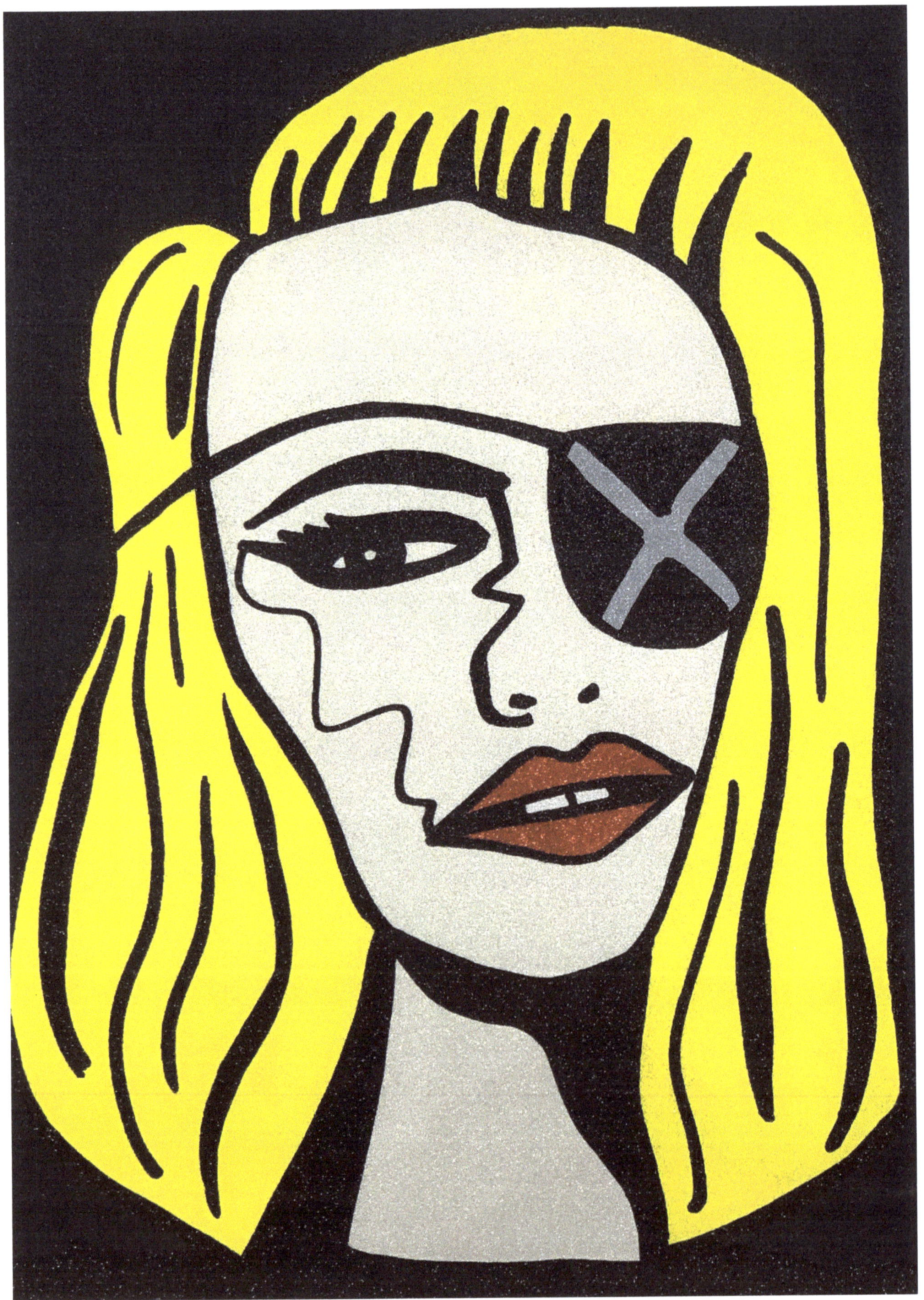

Illustration by Boy George

MEETING MADONNA

It's an absolute pleasure to meet you Madonna, I said
Even though I really don't know who you are
All I've been told is you're some sort of American pop star
Who's famous for being a virgin and wearing an oversized conical bra
I have no idea why I was invited to your end of tour party
But as you can I'm here so I turned up anyway
So why have I been ushered into this side room
And you're dressed like a princess and sitting on a throne chair
When there's hundreds of invited people waiting out there for you
By all accounts your tour has been very successful
But if you don't go outside and meet all your guests
This party will go down as the worst one in London ever
If all you're going to do is play at being a princess
And spend the evening sat on your stupid throne in this room

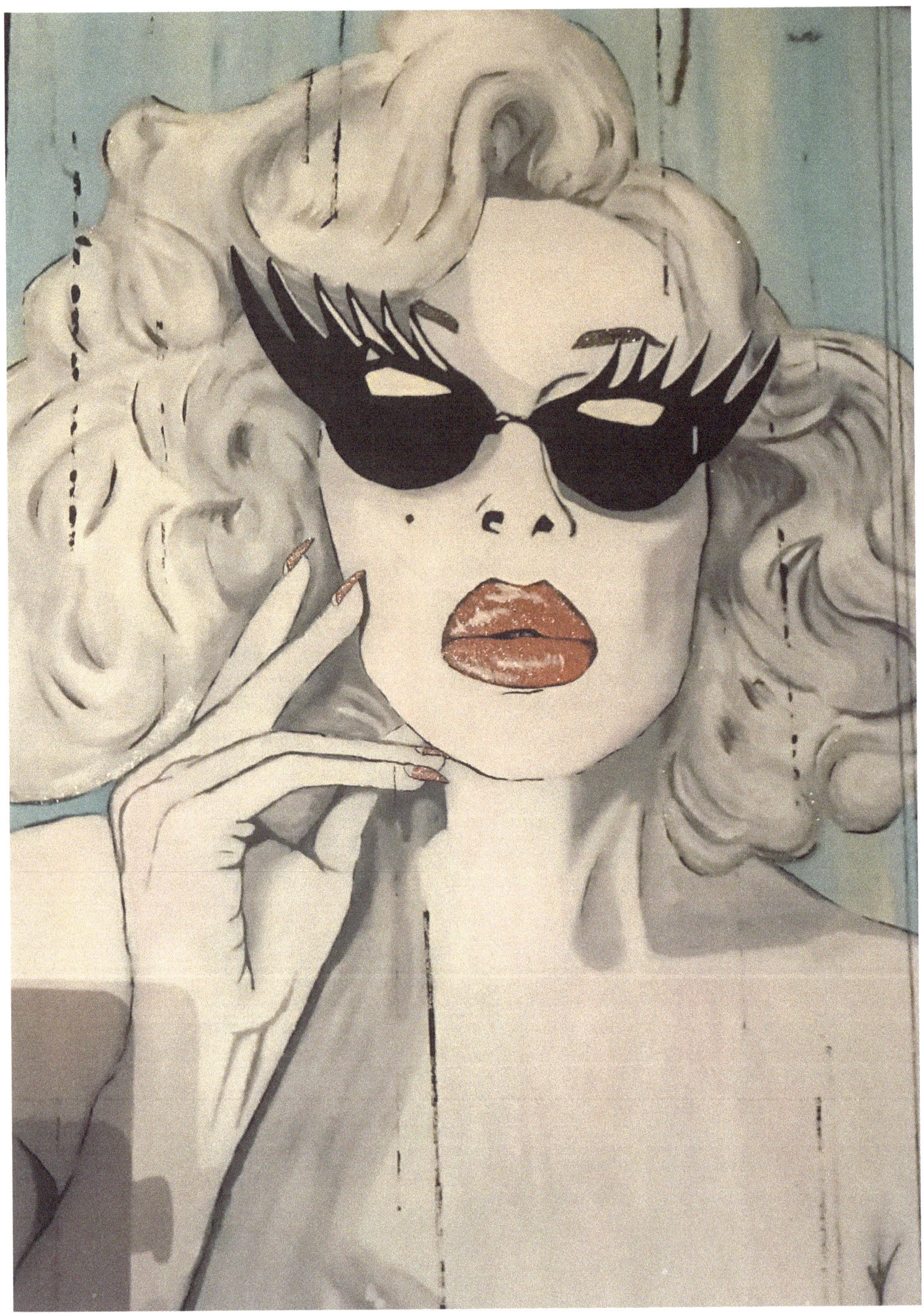

Illustration by Lena Nisula

MISS AMANDA LEPORE

She was a girl born a boy
So let me tell you more
This wasn't no ordinary woman
But the undisputed queen of New York
The incredibly fabulous iconic
One and only Miss Amanda Lepore
But when I say she's a queen
You can forget about drag
Having met her in person let me assure you
She is definitely a woman for sure
The bigger your dreams
The harder you'll have to fall
Unless of course you happen to be
Miss Amanda Lepore
To some she can be quite a bitch
To others a tart with a heart
Her humour could well be described
As brutally honest and even quite dark
But at the end of the day
No one can actually cast any doubt
That she was and still is an icon
To all LGBT people across the world
For putting herself up on offer
At a time when people like her
Faced bigotry, exclusion and even physical harm

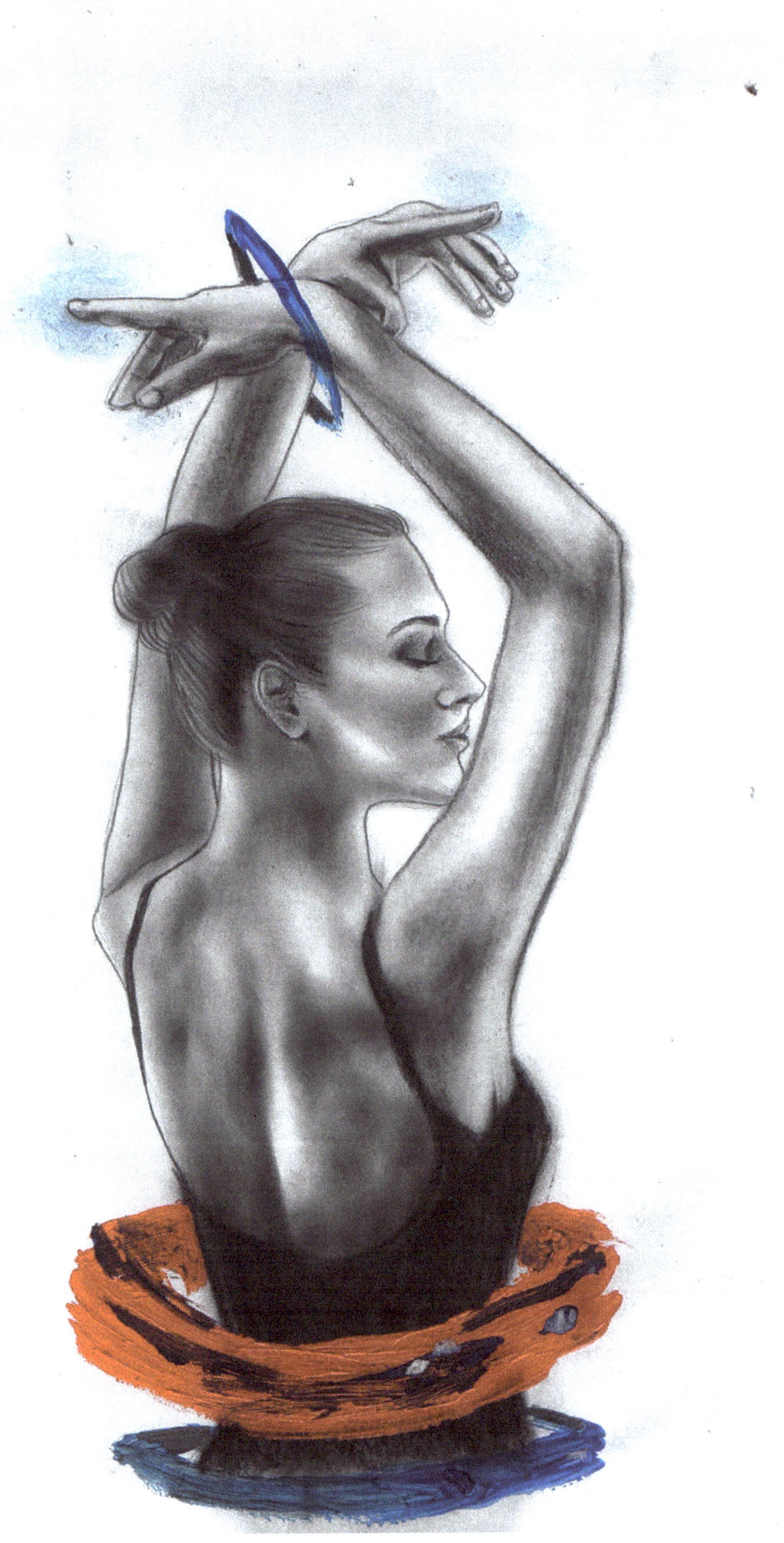

Illustration by Suzana Paula Bomfin

THAT ONE NIGHT STAND

Her kiss was like a spider's
The kind that lingers on a wall
Transparent and forgotten
Until she sees her victim fall
And yet the words she used
Weren't actually hollow
They were spun
Just like a perfect web
And I swear to God
That the world stood still
As she pulled me down
And climbed inside my head
But alas there was no time
For any kind of pillow talk
We shared just that one night
Together in my bed
A night of pure unbridled passion
Where nothing much was said
And when I woke up in the morning
She was nowhere to be seen
The only sign that she had even been there
Was a yellow post-it note with just three words
and XXX
Thank you darling kiss kiss kiss
Stuck to the headboard of my bed

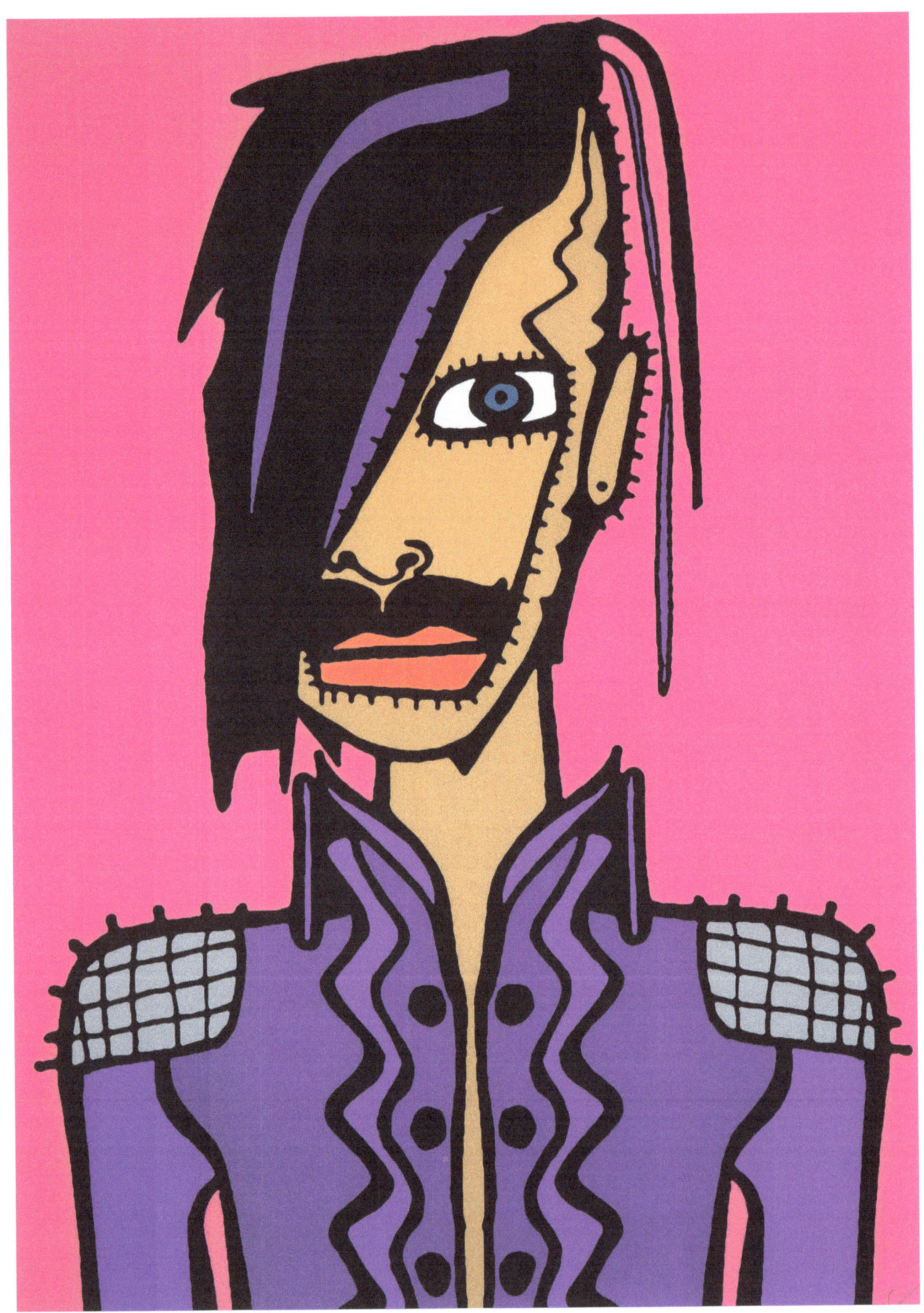

Illustration by Boy George

PURPLE PRINCE

Prince started off by wondering
What happens when doves cry
Whilst he was cruising round LA
In his little red corvette
When he spotted a rather pretty girl
And said I would die 4 u
Why would you do that she said
And he replied
Because you've got the look
And you're rather gorgeous too
He winked at her and said let's go crazy
She shook her head and said get off
Where're you going he said take me with you
If I was your girlfriend she replied I would
Ok he said do you want to live the pop life
Because I wanna be your lover
We can travel round America together
Even climb up mountains high
Let me tell you now girl I feel for you
Oh and by the way my name is Prince
Ok I'm going to call you the Cinnamon Girl
Prince and Cinnamon Girl yeah let's go to work
I want to hear you call my name
Because nothing compares to you
So let's see what happens in the future
I just want to do it all night
You and I creating thunder baby if that's alright

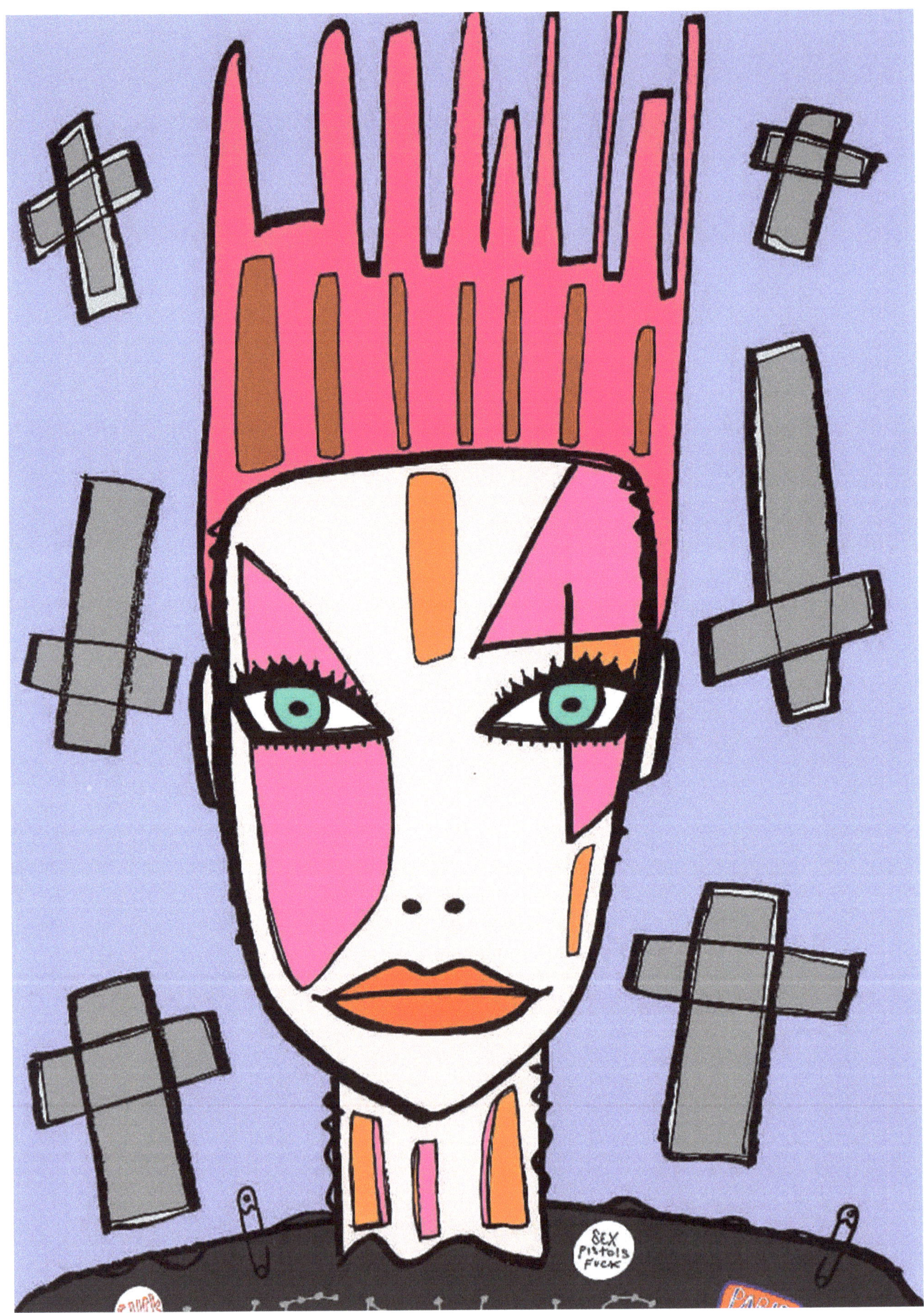

Illustration by Boy George

SHE KNOWS YOU KNOW

She'll walk in smiling
With the devil at her side
She'll wear the kinda smug expression
That says this bitch don't need to hide
She wears her disappointment
Like some medal on her chest
Then stands real proud
And whispers loud
Honey you don't pass my test
Everything about her
Screams out: Look at me
She will wear a different outfit
Just to steal the scene
She has an attitude with swagger
She's good at twisting words
She doesn't need to compromise
That would be absurd
She has her own agenda
That much is crystal clear
Not being the centre of attention
Is actually her greatest fear
She is a woman after all
And it is a man's world
So she ain't going to compromise
That ain't what she deserves
She's learnt how to play the game
From many different men
And she ain't going to settle
For second best again
She don't need anyone to tell her
She's got it all going on
So if you're looking for a trophy
You've got this woman wrong
Your arm ain't strong enough
To have her hanging on

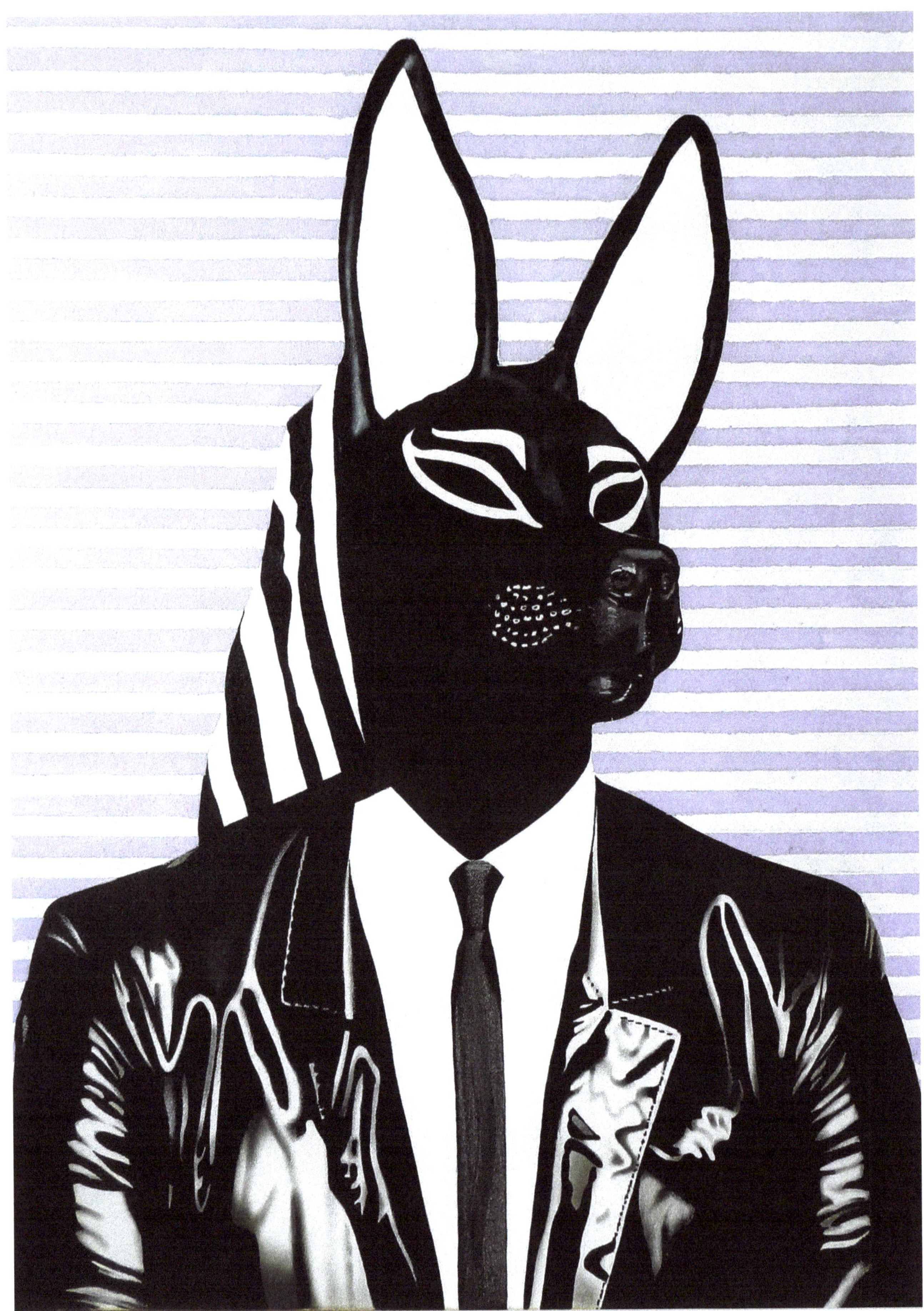

Illustration by Mark Wardel AKA TradeMark

THE WORLD OF MAKE BELIEVE

Step into my garden
Choose a ripple from my pool
You won't need to sit
And watch the flowers dying
Or have to listen to the birds
Sing out of tune
You and I could swim across
The deepest ocean
Climb the highest mountain
Reach up and touch the sky
We could even walk on water
If ever such a thought
Should cross our minds
I could take you to nirvana
Of course I know the way
I've been there before
And we won't need no powders
Pills or potions
To hear the thunder
Crash against our bedroom door
I could teach you how
To dance with shadows
Prove beyond all doubt
That you could live life on the edge
You could either choose
To hold the devil by the hand
Unless of course you would prefer
To have an angel share your bed
Because anything is possible
In the world of make believe
All it takes is some imagination
And the willingness to close your eyes
And actually take that leap
Which is something we already do
When we close our eyes to sleep
That's when we leave behind reality
And drift into a dream
A world of possibilities
Known as the world of make believe

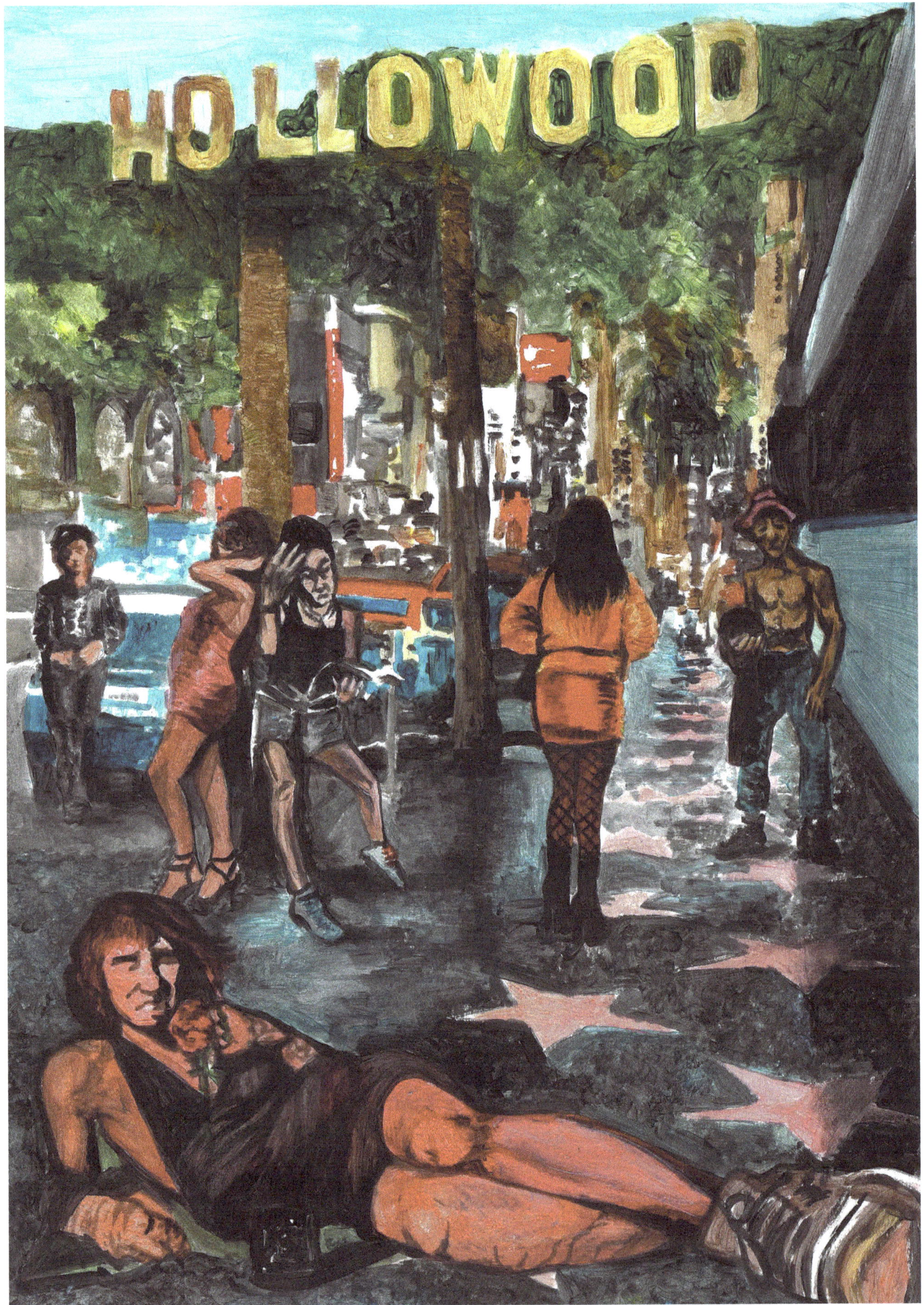

Illustration by Howard Priestley

HOLLYWOOD (City of Angels)

How can this be Hollywood
Isn't Hollywood already dead
Pick another movie babe
Or better still just take me back to bed
Everyone you meet's a star
They've got a stage in every street
Full bottle bleached blonde barbie dolls
That have to turn a trick to eat
In Hollywood the city of angels
A world of make believe
Hollywood's a fantasy
Built on promises and dreams
A city full of cocaine smiles
Where they love to stand
And watch each other bleed
Tinseltown has lost its shine
Now the dollar bill is god
Where bus boys in the coffee shops
Are dressed by Hugo Boss
There are tourists taking bus tours
Around the houses of the rich
The multi-million-dollar mansions
Where the A list movie stars all live
With super cars parked on the drive
That belong to high school kids
With their LVT monogrammed satchels
And diamond studded Rolex watches
on their wrists
There are people eating out of
garbage cans
Behind Michelin-starred restaurants
for dogs
Who have come in from the suburbs
Looking for a job
Chauffeur-driven limousines
Drop off ladies that lunch
For a coffee and gossip with their friends
Before they go off to rinse their husbands'
credit cards
On the latest must-have designer
handbags
At a mere fifty grand a pop
The movers and the shakers
Meet up for breakfast meetings
At the exclusive garden café
Pretending to be surprised
When they're targeted by the paps
The swanky shops on Rodeo Drive
Present an air of fantasy
A strip of sparkling facades
Camouflage the grim reality
That Hollywood's a city full of opulence
and excess
Surrounded by a sea of abject poverty

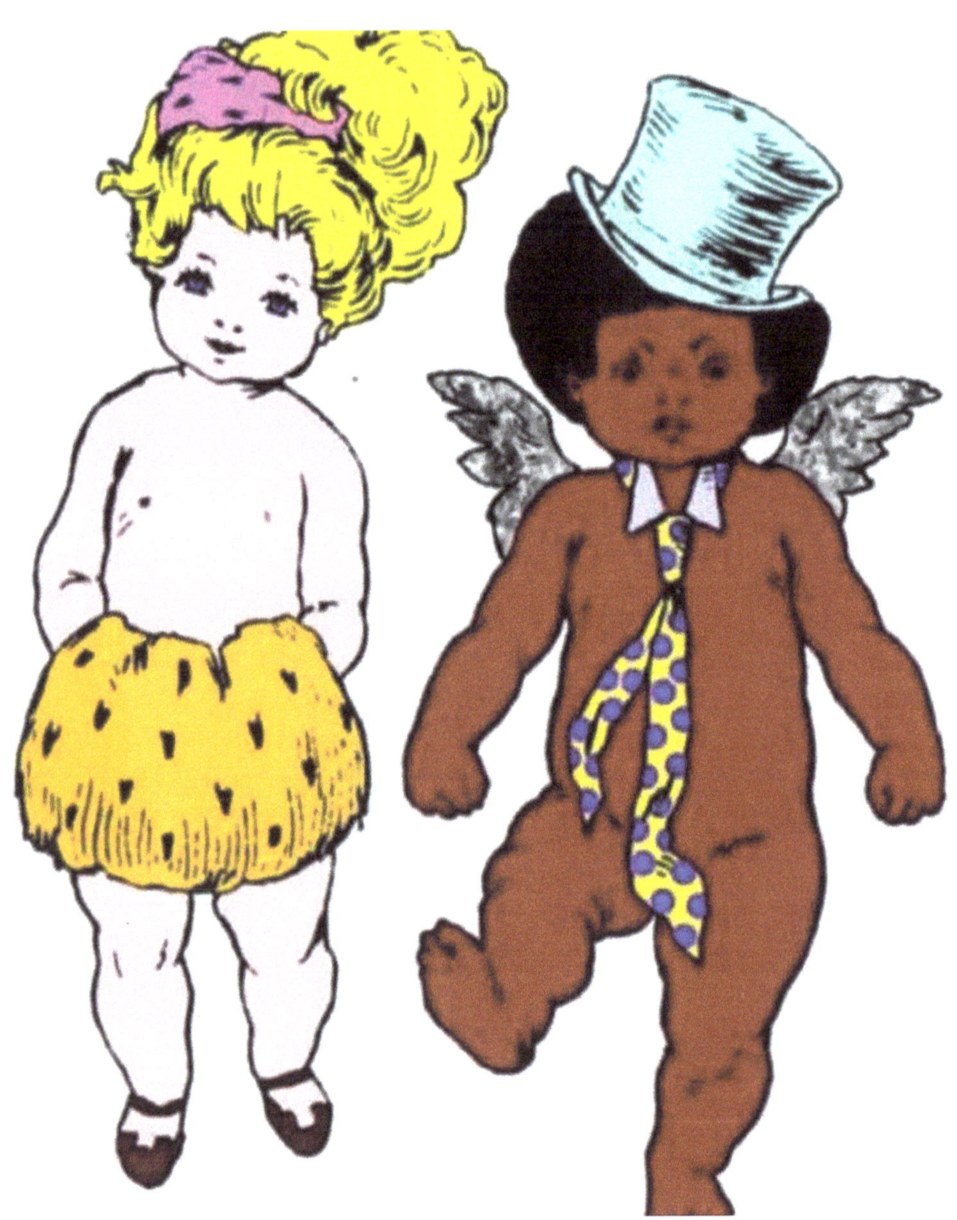

Illustration by Kevin O'Dowd

FALLING IN LOVE

Love is that stranger
You walked past on the street
It's that moment of madness
When your heart skips a beat
Love's an obsession
It's a shot in the dark
Love's the hand that you hold
As you stroll through the park
Love is a powerful drug
But it's a natural high
For some it's the reason for living
Whilst for others a reason to die
Love is that meeting of eyes
From across a crowded room
It stops you dead in your tracks
And makes your heart go boom
Love is an awkward moment
When you've got nothing to say
That moment of sheer panic
When somebody walks away
Love is all you really want
Just like everybody else
It's that photo of someone you've lost
That sits proudly on a shelf

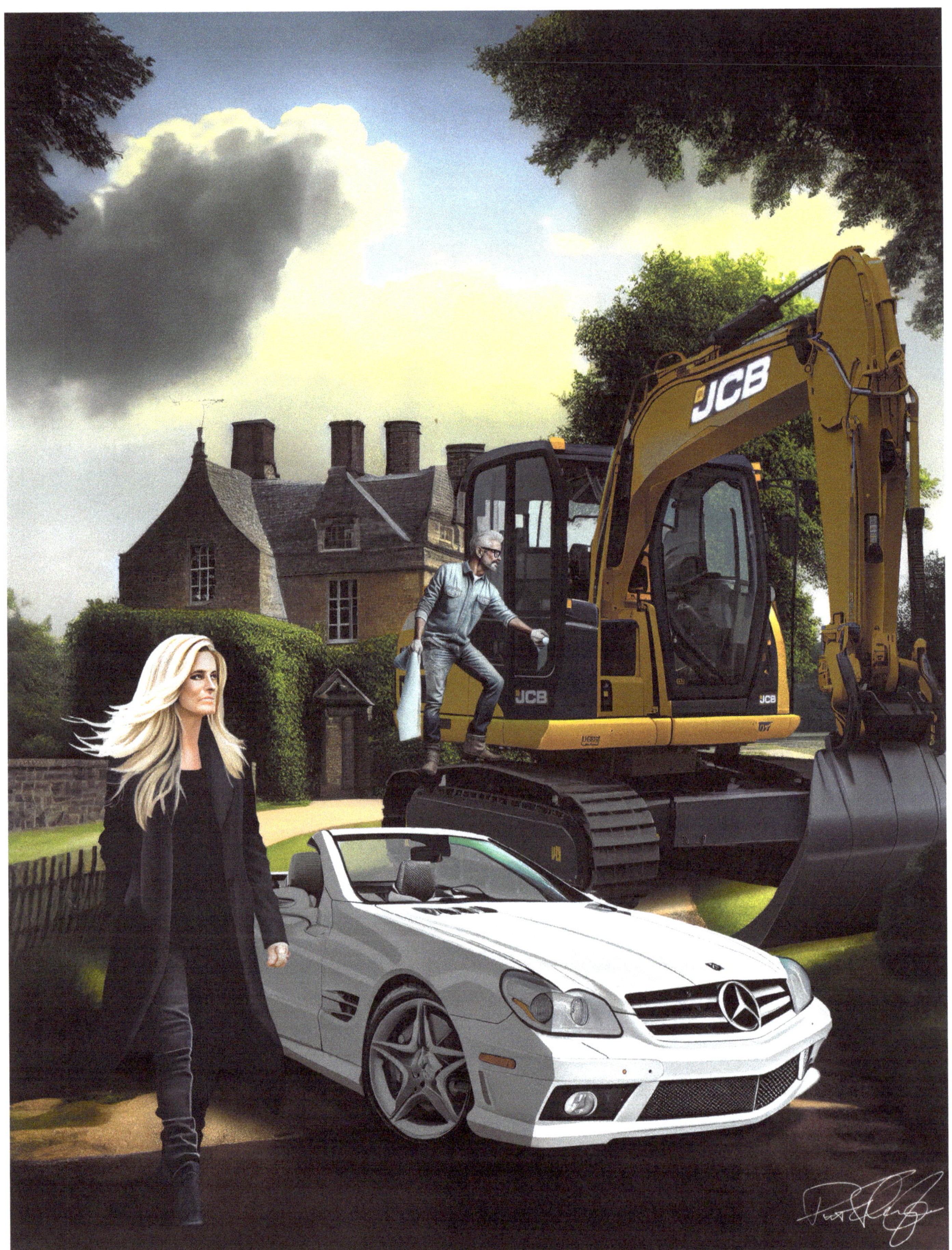

Illustration by Pat Flanagan

AMANDA AND BOB

Right, you're not coming out with me looking like that
Now get back up those stairs and get changed
What on earth made you think of wearing those jeans out to dinner?
Off you go, hurry up and get changed: you do not want to make me late
We're having dinner with Malcolm and Ruth tonight remember
So I'm telling you now Bobby Boy you do not want to misbehave
If you show me up tonight Bobby Boy you'll live to regret it
And you can forget about going out Friday night with the boys ok
Oh and nobody wants to hear about your bloody new yellow digger either
In fact it's best you say nothing unless I ask you a question ok
And we're going to dinner at the new Italian restaurant on Broad Street
So don't even think about trying to order burger and chips again
And they don't have bloody Tennent's Extra on tap as well you know
So there's a six pack for you in the fridge for later but only if you behave
So put on the Hugo Boss suit, your Kurt Geiger shoes
And the white shirt I've left out on the bed
And just be quick about it please because I don't want to be bloody late
Oh and you can leave your new 32 ton digger at work from now on
I do not want to see it parked on the drive next my Mercedes again

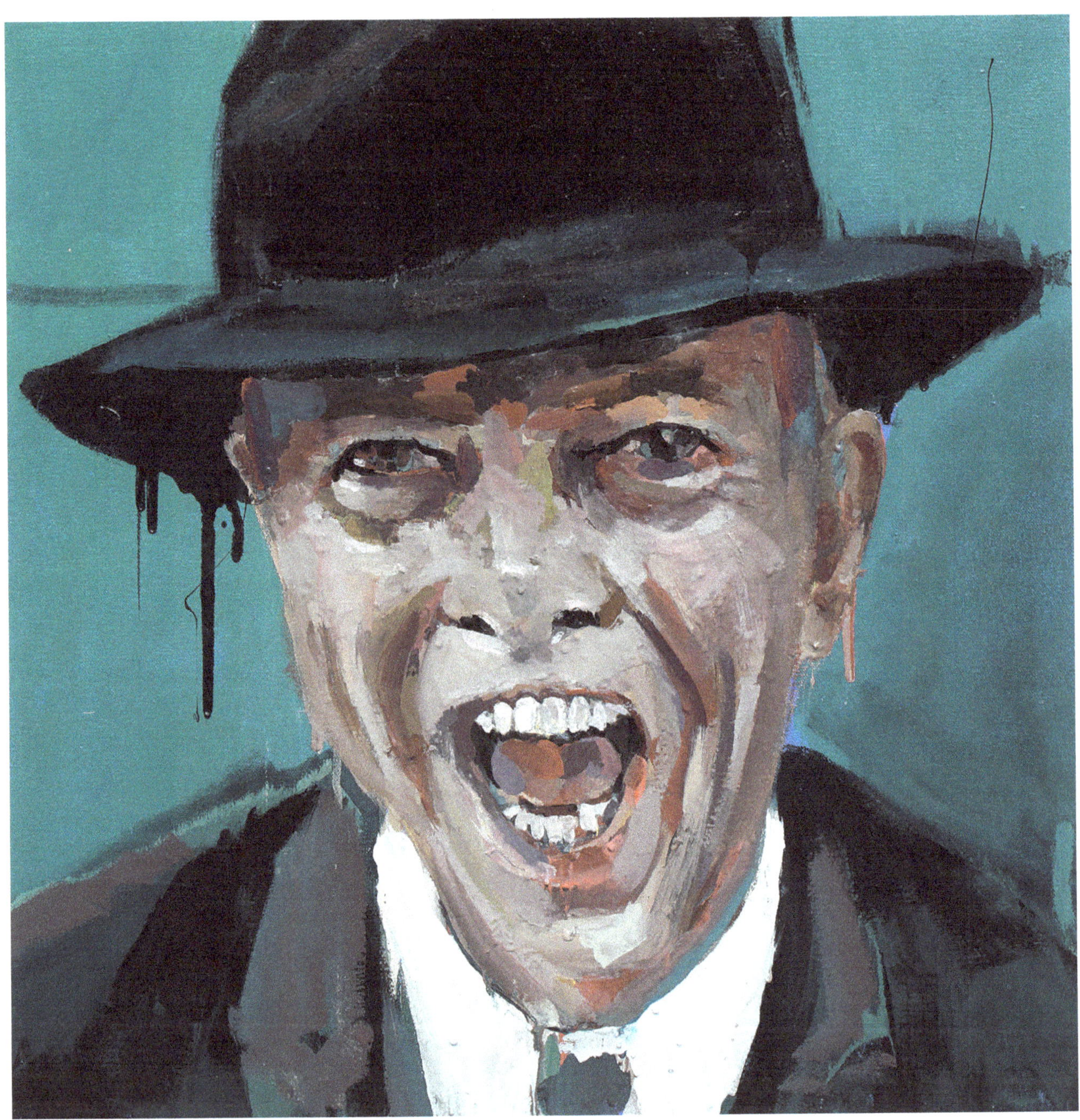

Illustration by Julie Bennett
Bowie
2019
Oil on canvas
56 x 56 cm
(Available as a limited edition print from www.juliebennett.co.uk)

DAVID

David Bowie was someone who definitely stood out from the crowd
A man who had something to say without having to open his mouth
From spiders from Mars to a girl who wore red shoes
He was a international superstar who managed to capture the mood
He was hunky dory, Major Tom and the man who fell to earth
A man who was destined to become a pop star from his birth
In a career that spanned several decades
He was a pivotal part of generations of people's youths
Producing five decades of innovative groundbreaking music
Whilst always remaining true to his working class roots
But he was so much more than just a fabulous musician
He was an artist, fashionista and a Hollywood movie star
A lyricist, poet and passionate campaigner for human rights
A truly genuine twentieth/twenty-first century icon
Who was sadly taken away from us all far too early in life

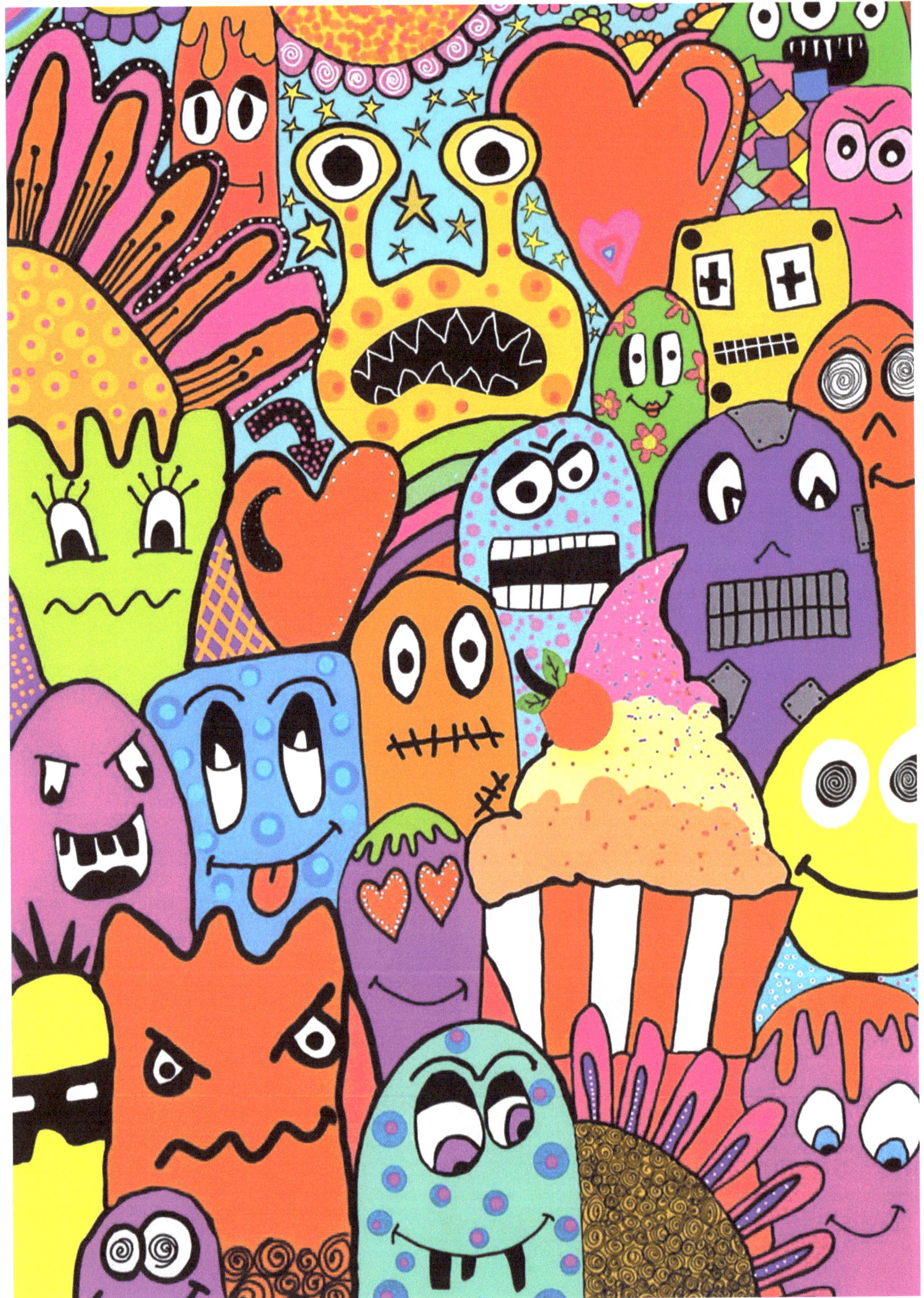

Illustration by Sean George

ALWAYS AN ALTERNATIVE

Anyone can lead a horse to water
But once you get it there
You cannot force that horse to drink
But you can always push the stubborn git into a river
And I guarantee if it don't start to swim
It's absolutely gonna sink
They say that those who choose to lay with dogs
Have no right to complain if they end up catching fleas
But I'm not sure that's going to bother many men
If like a dog they can lick their own bits and pieces as and when they please
It is often said that one should never burn bridges
So instead of making rash decisions one should stop and count to ten
Which actually makes a lot of sense to be quite honest
Cos if you cross the Thames from south to north
You soon bloody want to go back south again
They say that if you come across a mountain that's too high to climb
You can simply walk around it to reach the other side
But personally I wouldn't bother doing either to be honest
I'd simply save my pennies up because if I had to get from A to B I'd bleeding fly
All I'm actually trying to say is that there's always an alternative
So whenever you hit any kind of problem you can always find another way to sort it out
I just usually give up and just go straight back bed as soon I start having any doubts
Because as we all know it isn't going to take too long anyway
Before some clever sod will get to work the problem out

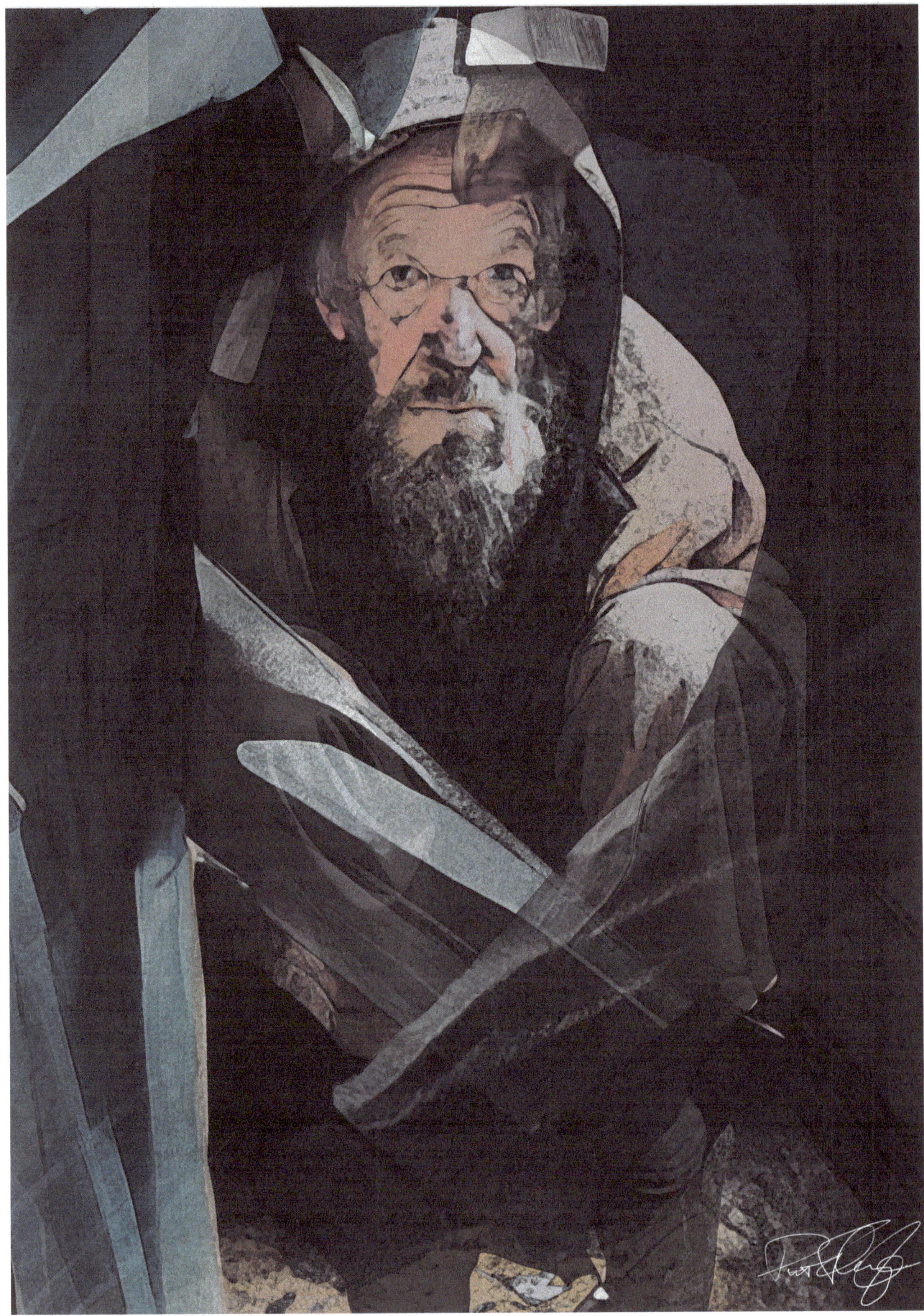

Illustration by Pat Flanagan

NO PLACE FOR THE OLD

You're walking around
On feet made of clay
Shouting at shadows
With nothing to say
You're venting frustrations
You demand to be heard
But all that you're doing
Is frightening the birds
You're shuffling your feet
Staring down at the ground
Surrounded by people
Yet all alone in the crowd
People walk past you
With barely a glance
While you're asking yourself
Why won't they give me a chance
An old lady approaches
And hands you some coins
Her compassionate smile
Cuts straight through the noise
As the darkness descends
And the streets empty out
The world becomes calmer
When there's no one about
You need to find shelter
You're feeling the cold
As you suddenly realise
This is no place for the old
As you lay in a doorway
You shiver and shake
Mulling over your failures
And all your past mistakes
If only you'd known
What you know now
Life may have been different
To how it's worked out
You used to be loved
You had people who cared
But when you couldn't cope
They all ran away scared
They knew you had problems
But then they had their own
And unfortunately that kind of loyalty
Ain't always carved into stone
As you seek to find shelter
From the cruel bitter winds
You start to remember
Your many past sins
All the people you hurt
With no intention in mind
The people who loved you
That have left you behind
You feel sad and lonely
And you're crying inside
But you won't shed real tears
You've got far too much pride
You need to find shelter
You're feeling the cold
As you suddenly realise
This is no place for the old

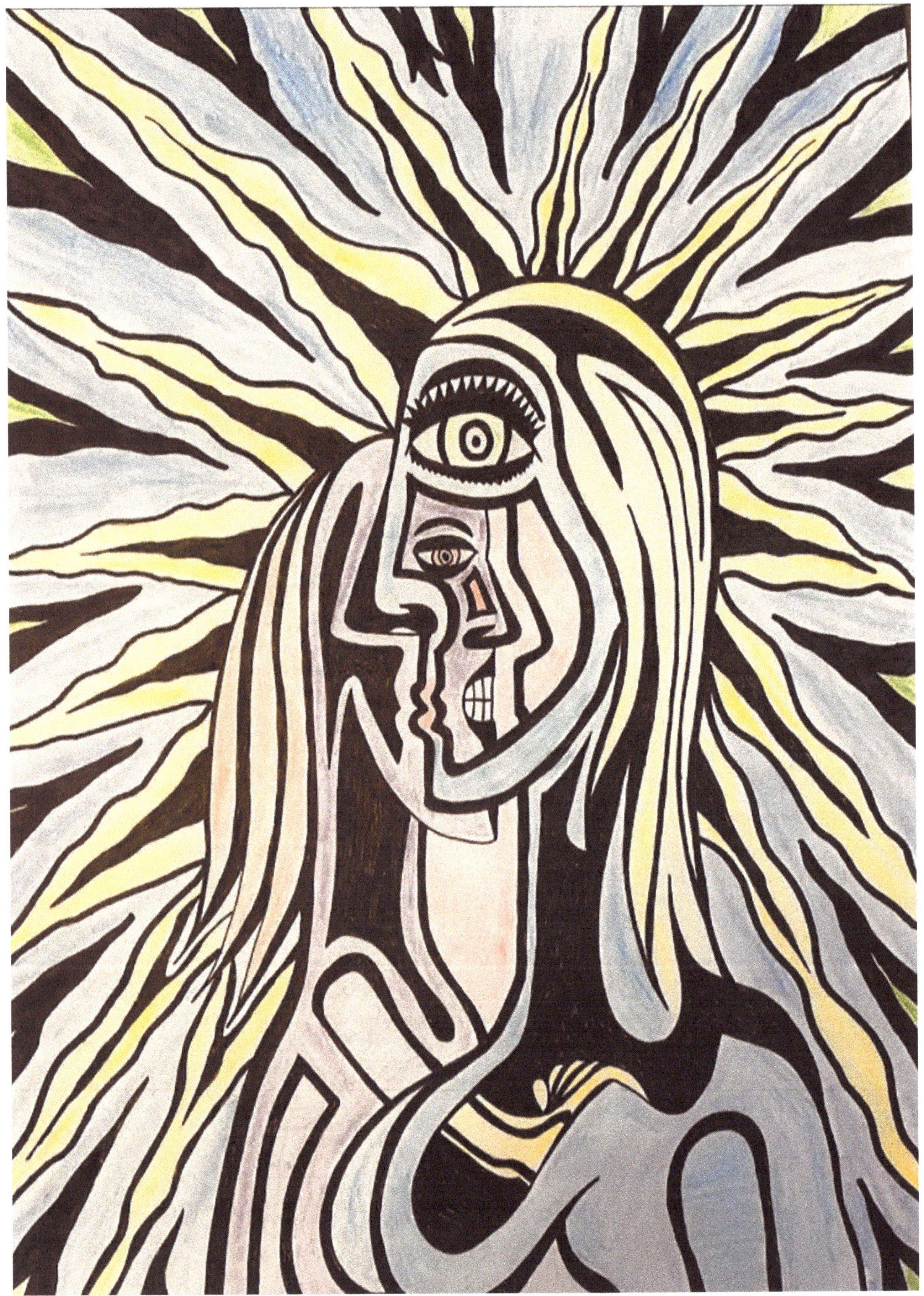

Illustration by Albert Haines

ARE YOU FOR REAL?

Who the hell are you
To question my morality
And then presume to offer me
Your unsolicited opinions and advice
And even if I was in need
Of someone else's counsel
What makes you think I'd turn to you
To help me put the world to rights
Why on earth would I need
To ask for your approval
Considering that your concerns
Are actually irrelevant to me
In fact I'd say you lost
Any right that you may once have had
To question my decisions
The moment you decided
That you would lie and cheat
But apart from all the obvious
Such as I flipping hate your guts
I find you very tiresome
Rude, arrogant and totally obnoxious
And although it pains me not
To actually have to say this
You've also got the kind of face
That I would really love to punch

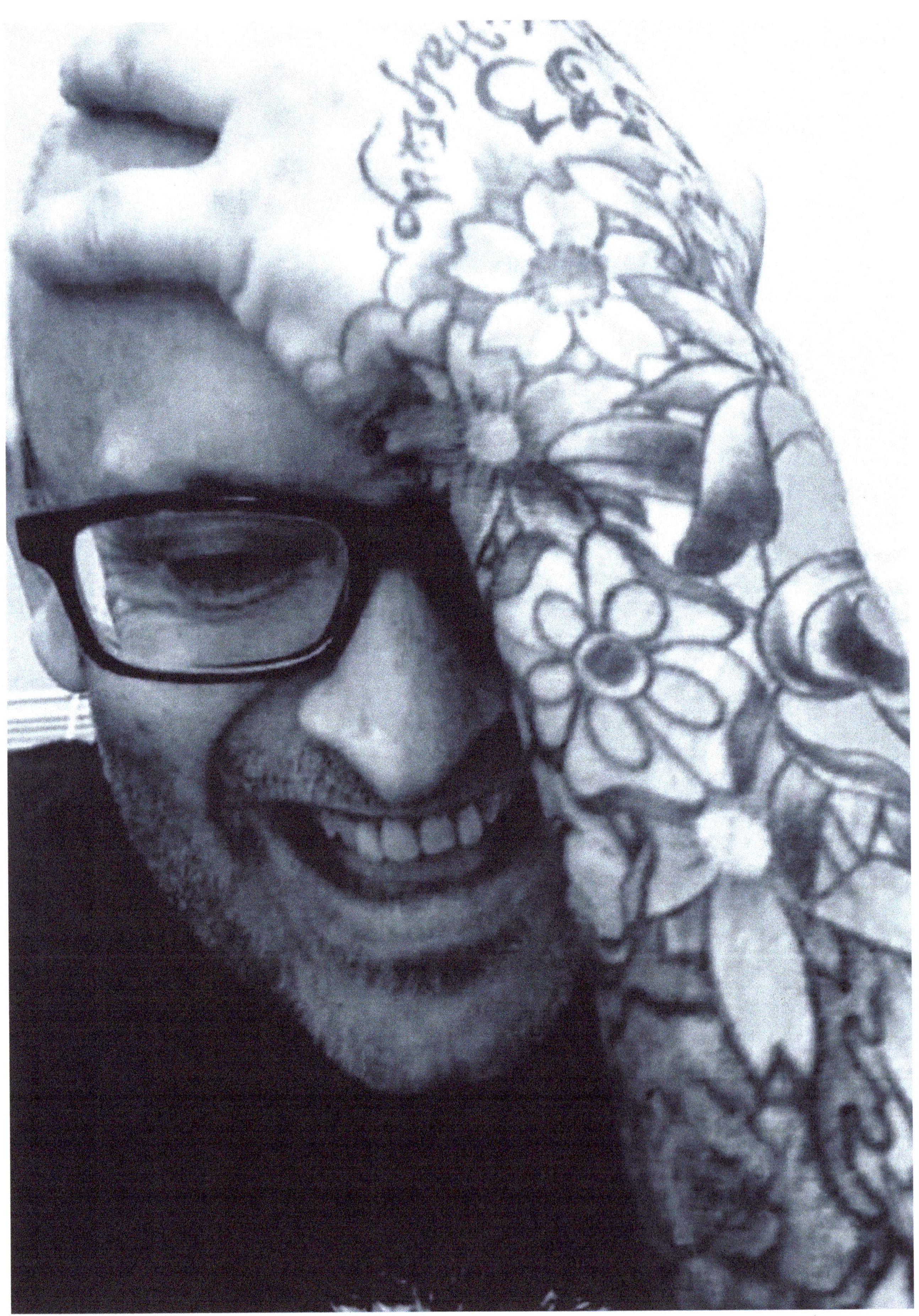

SH#T HAPPENS

Everybody has their own
Particular agenda
As well as their personal
Opinions and beliefs
And not everyone can actually be right at the same time
And unfortunately things can often lead to violence between those who disagree
There is so much in life we question
Without answers
And yet there are even more things that are neither wrong or right
And although most of us accept that sh#t is going to happen
There are those who choose to turn to God
In the hope that he'll provide a guiding light
Life can sometimes be such a bitter disappointment
And even more so should things turn out not to be
Either quite as you had maybe once envisaged
Or the total opposite of everything that you had perhaps believed
So I guess the moral to this story if indeed there is one
Is maybe that iconic cub scout motto: be prepared
In other words accept that sometimes things just simply don't work out
But then that doesn't necessarily mean
That just because something's been broken that it can't be repaired

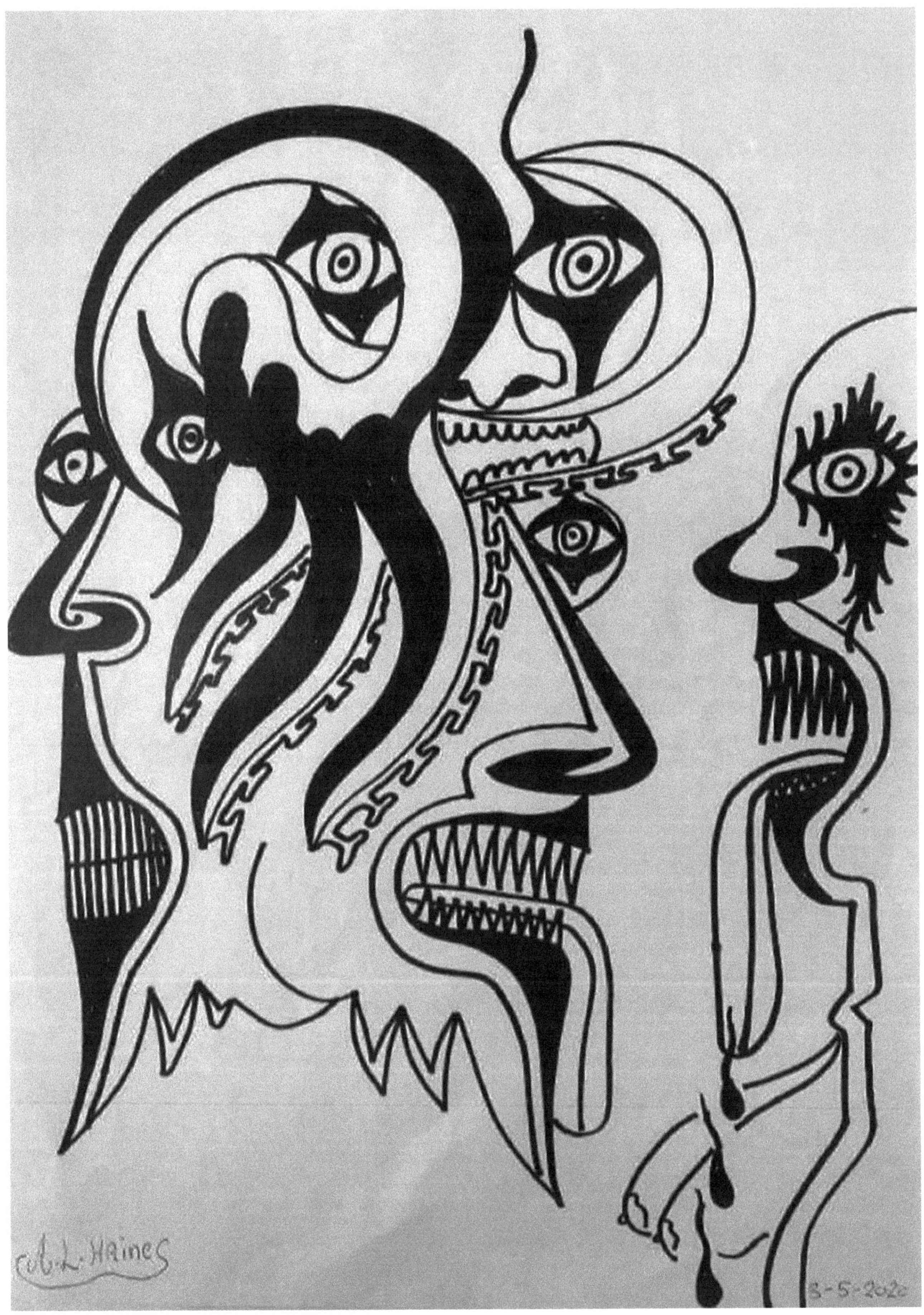

Illustration by Albert Haines

I LOST YOU TO COCAINE

To Kathy.

Stop walking in my shadows
Bouncing off the walls
Expecting me to pick you up
Every time you take a fall
I'm done with all your promises
How it's all a big mistake
I'm leaving you tomorrow
I've already packed my case
You should have made
More of an effort
Maybe even tell the truth
If you really were that worried
That I might cut you loose
It wasn't that I didn't love you
Even though you broke my heart
In the end it was the drugs
That tore us both apart
It was all down to white powder
That so-called party drug
A little line of cheap cocaine
Proved more powerful than love

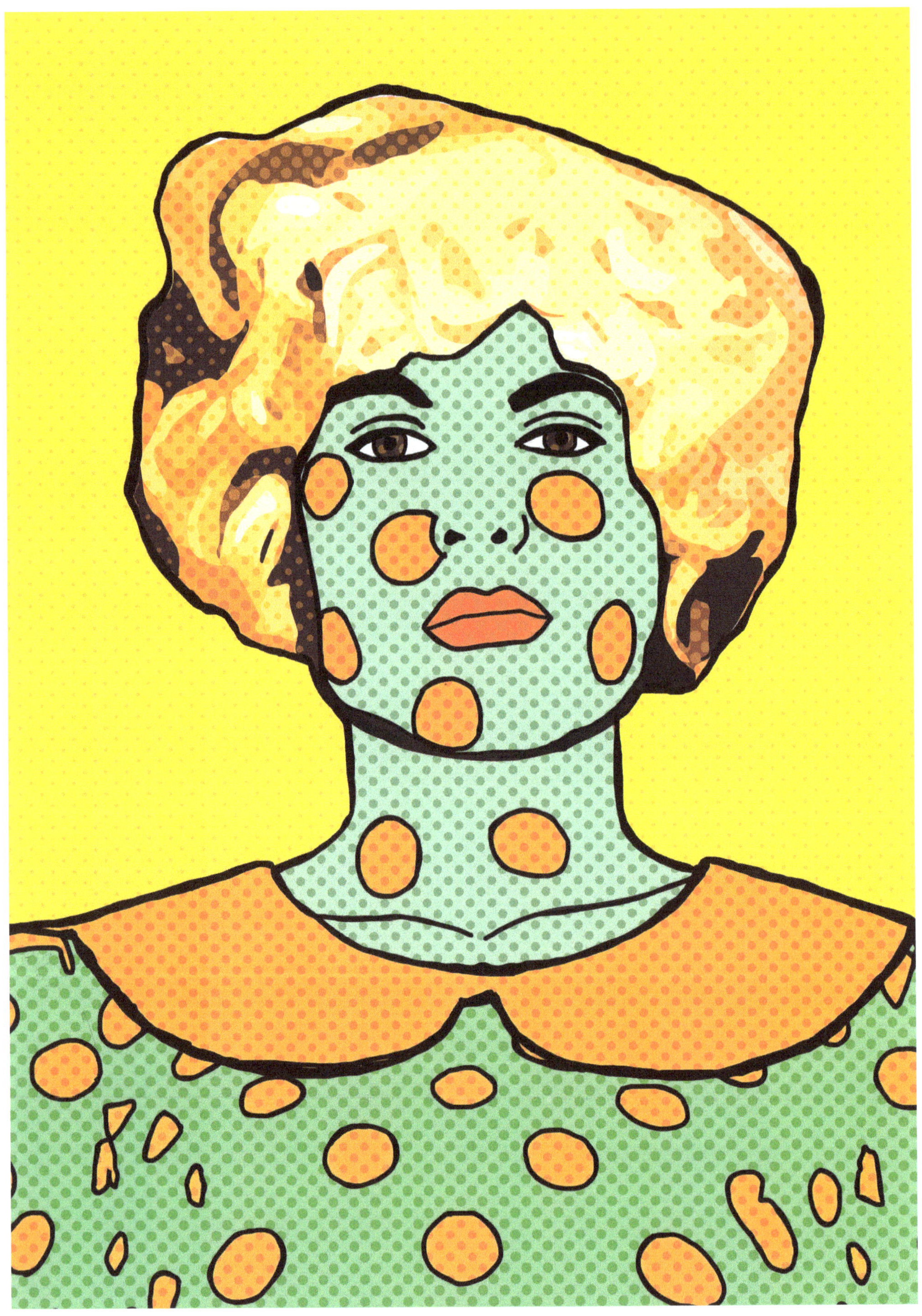

Illustration by Dean Stockings

LEIGH BOWERY

To some he was just parody
To others he was walking art
Often rather confrontational
But always very clever and quite smart
He was a cutting edge designer
A performance artist extraordinaire
Once defecating on his audience
Whilst suspended by a harness in the air
He would walk along the street wearing a toilet round his neck
In defiance of his critics who he felt had no respect
But then he really didn't actually care to be quite honest
In fact he once told me he couldn't give a monkey's chuff
He actually didn't use those actual words I have to say
It's just the words he used, even in a poetic form, may well be a bit too much
He was in my opinion a creative genius
And in the true sense of the word a bona fide influencer
Whose untimely death was not only a tragedy but a loss to all mankind
I feel it was a pleasure and an honour to have actually known him and have him as a friend
And the likes of people like Leigh Bowery only come along a few times in our lives

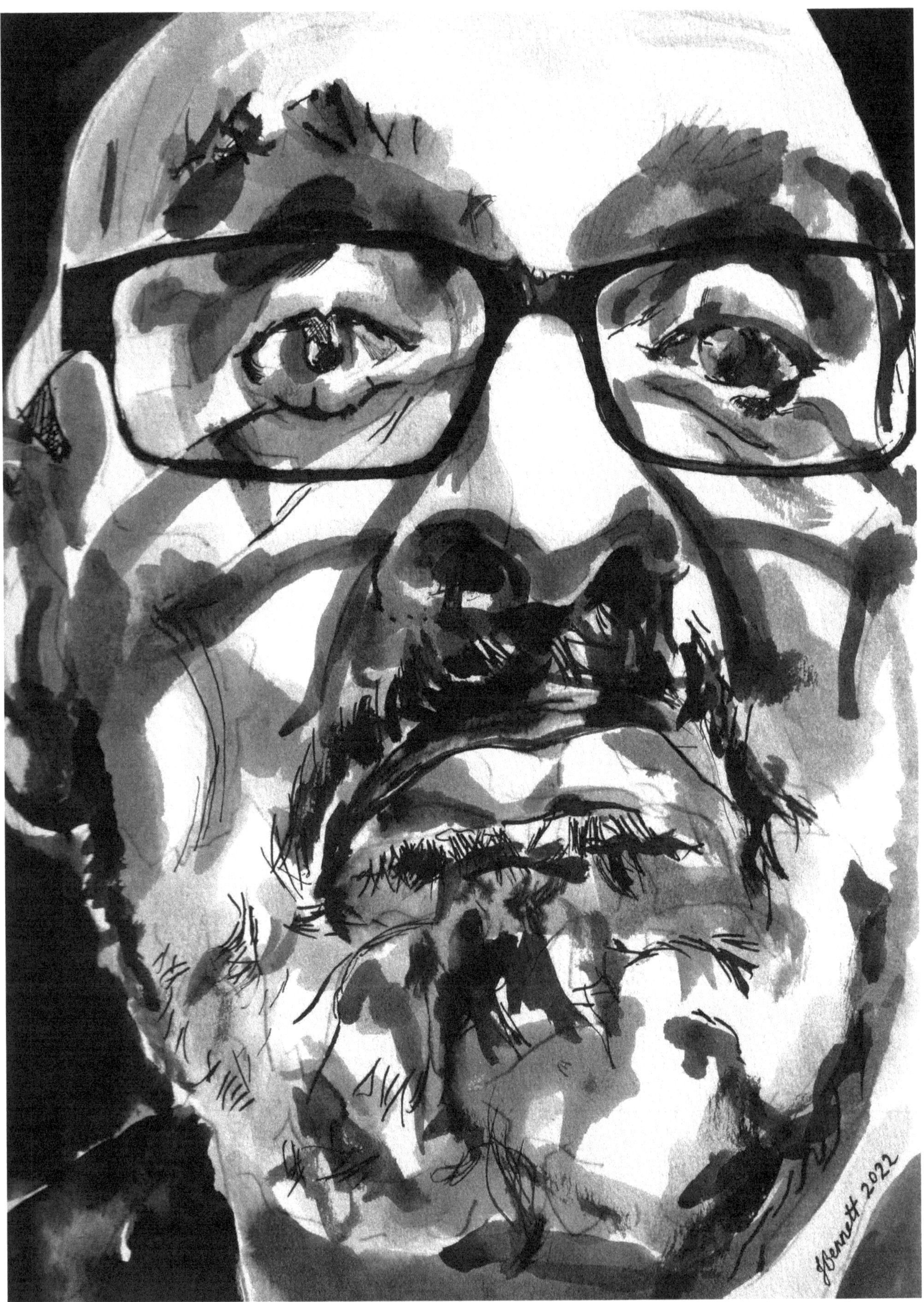

Illustration by JULIE BENNETT
Kevin O'Dowd 2022 Ink on board 22.7 x 30.4 cm

OUR PLANET IS DYING

Our planet is dying
But why should I care?
By the time it implodes
I ain't going to be there
I don't have any children
That I'll be leaving behind
And as for possessions
There won't be any to find
I live on the top of a hill
So flooding won't affect me
My back garden has been
Completely paved over
So I won't have to save
Any endangered trees
The hole in the ozone layer
Is no concern of mine
And as for the temperature rising
I actually like a bit of sunshine
The price of food has gone up
But I've got an Aldi
Just up the road
And I've bypassed
The gas meter anyway
So I won't be affected
By harsh winter cold
I've got a free bus pass as well
So I don't really need a car
And these days
I usually can't be arsed
To actually travel that far
I haven't bothered setting up
An over fifty's funeral plan either
Well I really don't see why
I should actually have to pay
And I'd much rather let someone else
Foot the bill for that anyway
I've got my collection of watches
Which I'm planning to sell pretty soon
And I'll be spending the money
All on myself actually
Yep that's exactly what I'm gonna do
I don't want to leave behind nothing
So all my possessions
Will be put up for sale
No one's done me any favours in life
So no one can actually complain
Well they can but it won't bother me
Cos I'll be bloody long dead anyway
The thing is why should I care
I won't be around actually
So when the earth finally implodes
It won't bloody bother me

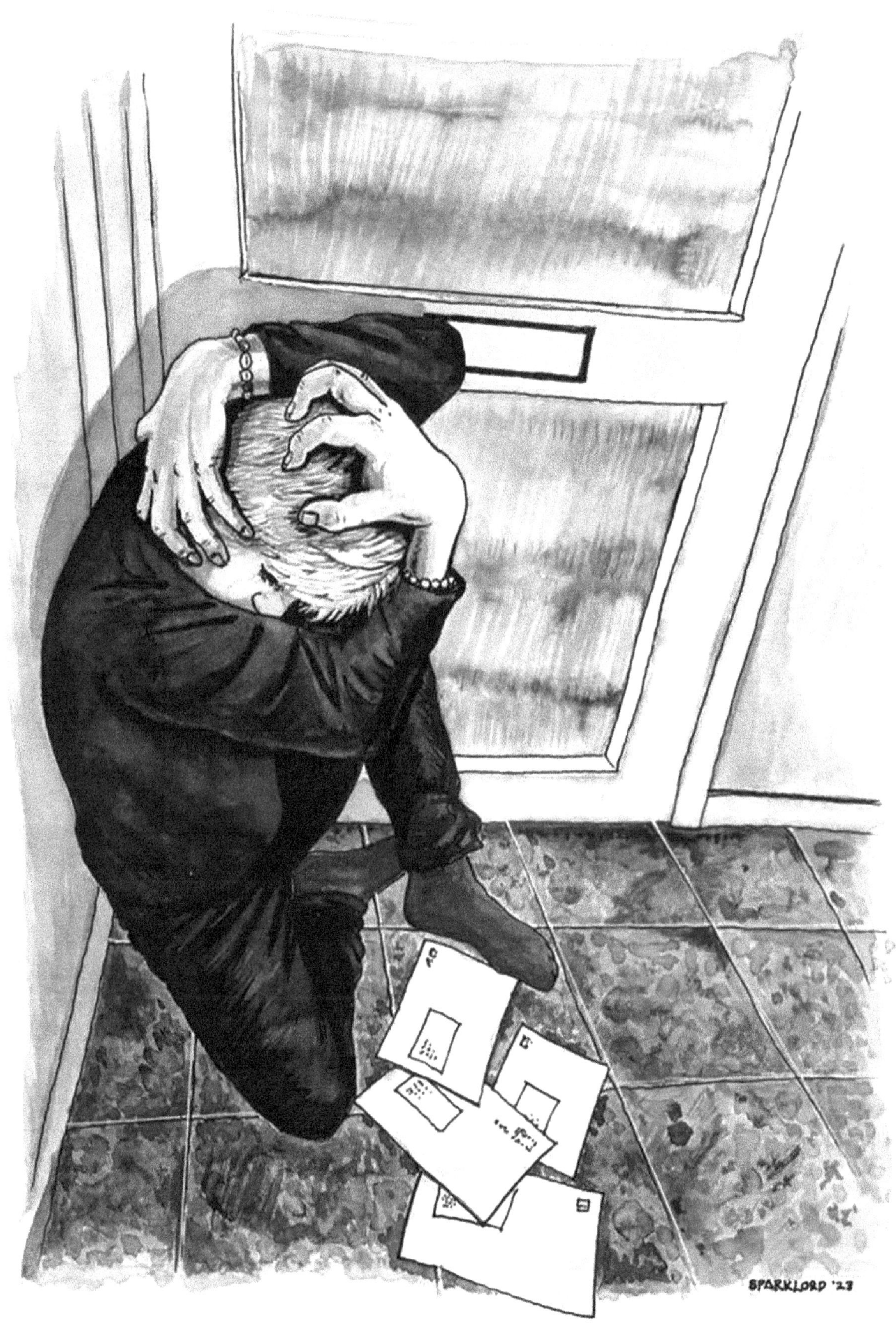

Illustration by Mark Campbell

SAVE ME FROM MYSELF

Need someone to save me
Save me from myself
Cos the way I've been playing
Ain't no good for my health
I've been partying all night
And sleeping all day
And now I'm up to my neck
With bills I need to pay
Need someone to save me
I'm about to fall hard
Been playing poker with life
From a marked deck of cards
Been leaving letters unopened
Hoping they'd go away
Now the bailiffs come knocking
On my door every day
I've been robbing Peter
So I can pay Paul
But I've forgotten to keep
My eye on the ball
The landlord's been calling
Demanding his rent
By the end of the month
Home could well be a tent
Need someone to save me
Save me from myself
Cos the way I've been playing
Ain't no good for my health
I've been telling myself
That I must pay my bills
Just one more night out
Then I'll stay home and chill
But then there's another big party
Everyone else will be there
And the next thing I know
I'm on the way out the door
And checking my hair

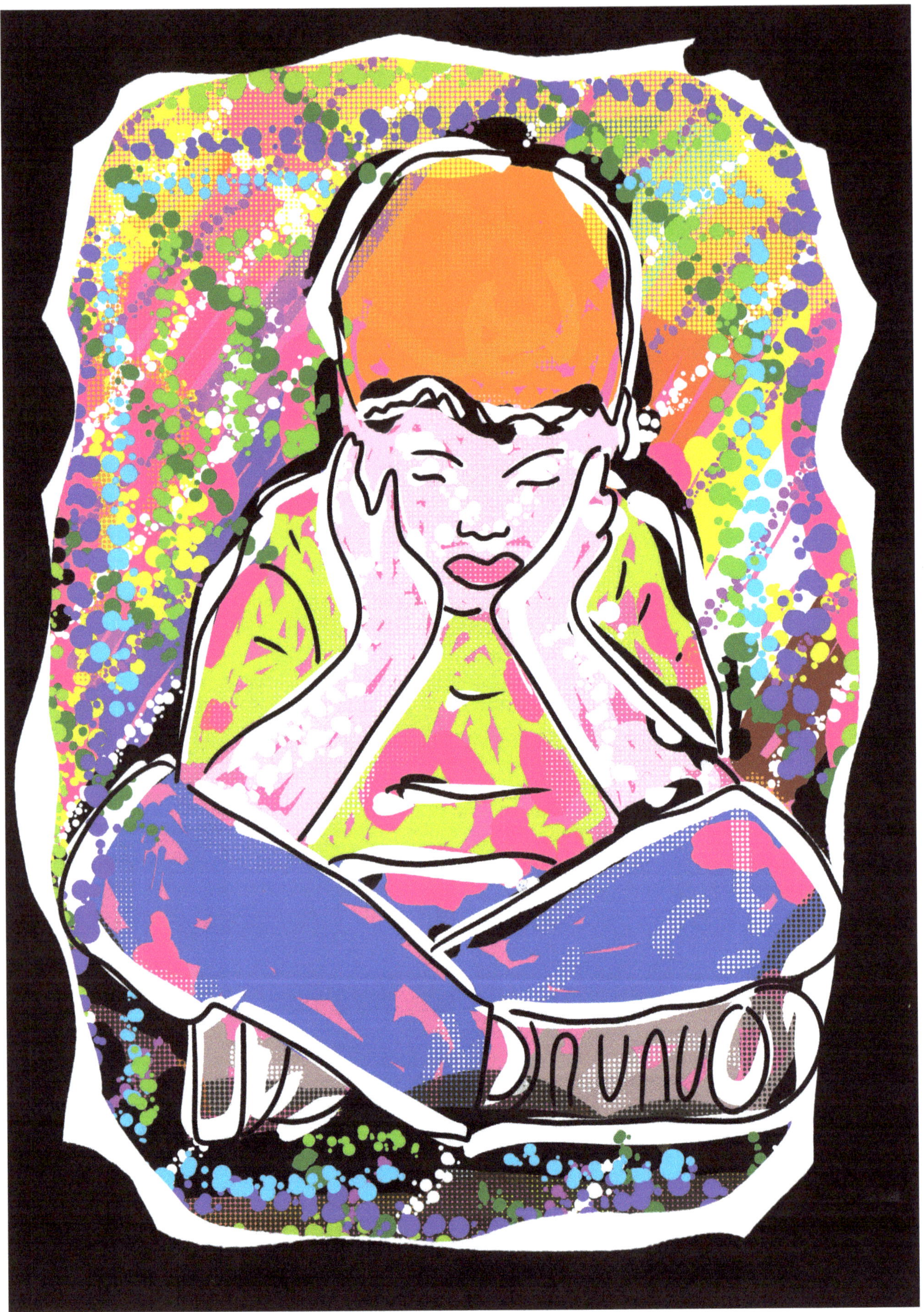

Illustration by Dusty O.

THE BOY WHO SAT BY THE WINDOW

The boy who sat by the window
Watching the world go by
People of every colour, race, religion and gender
From all different walks of life
Designer dreads shaking nylon heads
Sucking air through gold embellished teeth
Wannabe yardies with exaggerated swaggers
Bumping fists with each other as they meet
Single mothers weighed down with shopping
Struggling to control their stubborn three-year-olds
Spotting a nervous young couple on their first date
As he sat watching their romance unfold
A group of schoolgirls meet up on the corner
And start pulling their skirts up above their knees
Spot a cute boy walking past on the pavement
Before forming a huddle and starting to scream
Ladies who lunch meet up for a coffee and gossip
Sitting outside the bistro across the street
Before heading off to rinse their husbands' gold cards
In Kensington High Street's exclusive boutiques
A couple of local wide boys dressed head to toe in snide Armani
Hug each other in a well rehearsed gangster style
Watched by a real old school villain sat on a bench
Who rolls his eyes, nods his head and smiles
The edgy and avant-garde fashionistas and peacocks
Start appearing on the street alongside the maybes and really-not-sures
The desperately upwardly mobile and the usual array of wannabes
While the boy who sat by the window
Sat there watching while drinking a cup of tea

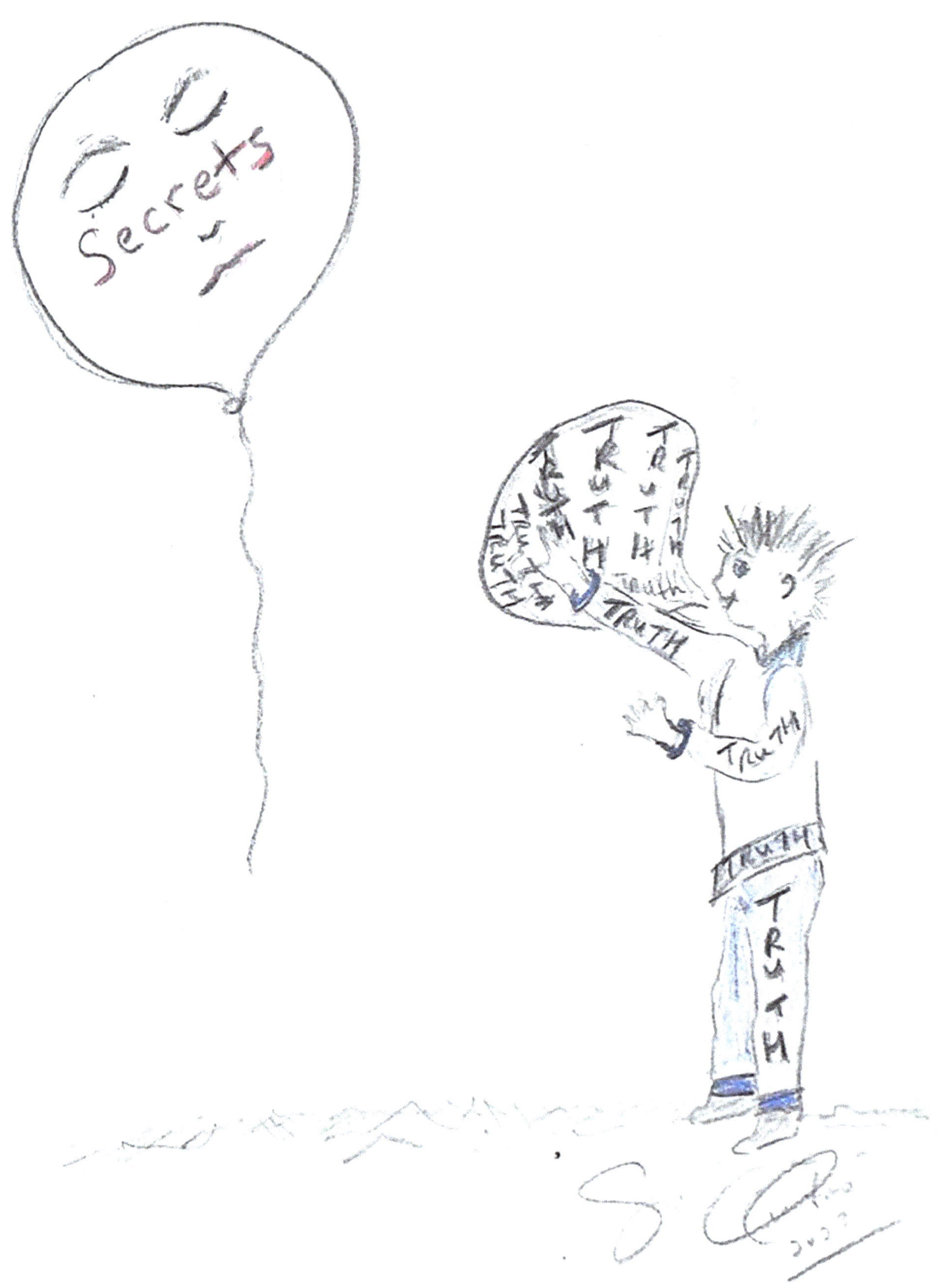

Illustration by Suzi Quatro

SECRETS

We all have our secrets
Something no one else knows
We've all made mistakes
That we don't want exposed
We're not being deceitful
Just protecting our pride
That's what we all do
When we've got something to hide
We've promised to do things
That just slipped our minds
We blame someone else
We've all done that at times
Those excuses we've made
Trying to get out of things
Like my battery was flat
I didn't hear the phone ring
Some say it's half truths
Others call it white lies
But it makes others think
You've got something to hide
And if you tell the truth
And admit your mistakes
Some people will choose
To throw it back in your face
But at the end of the day
The truth always comes out
So you'd best get in first
To erase any doubts
Because holding onto a secret
Can often just weigh you down
Remember some people
Like nothing better
Than being able to stand there
And watch while you drown

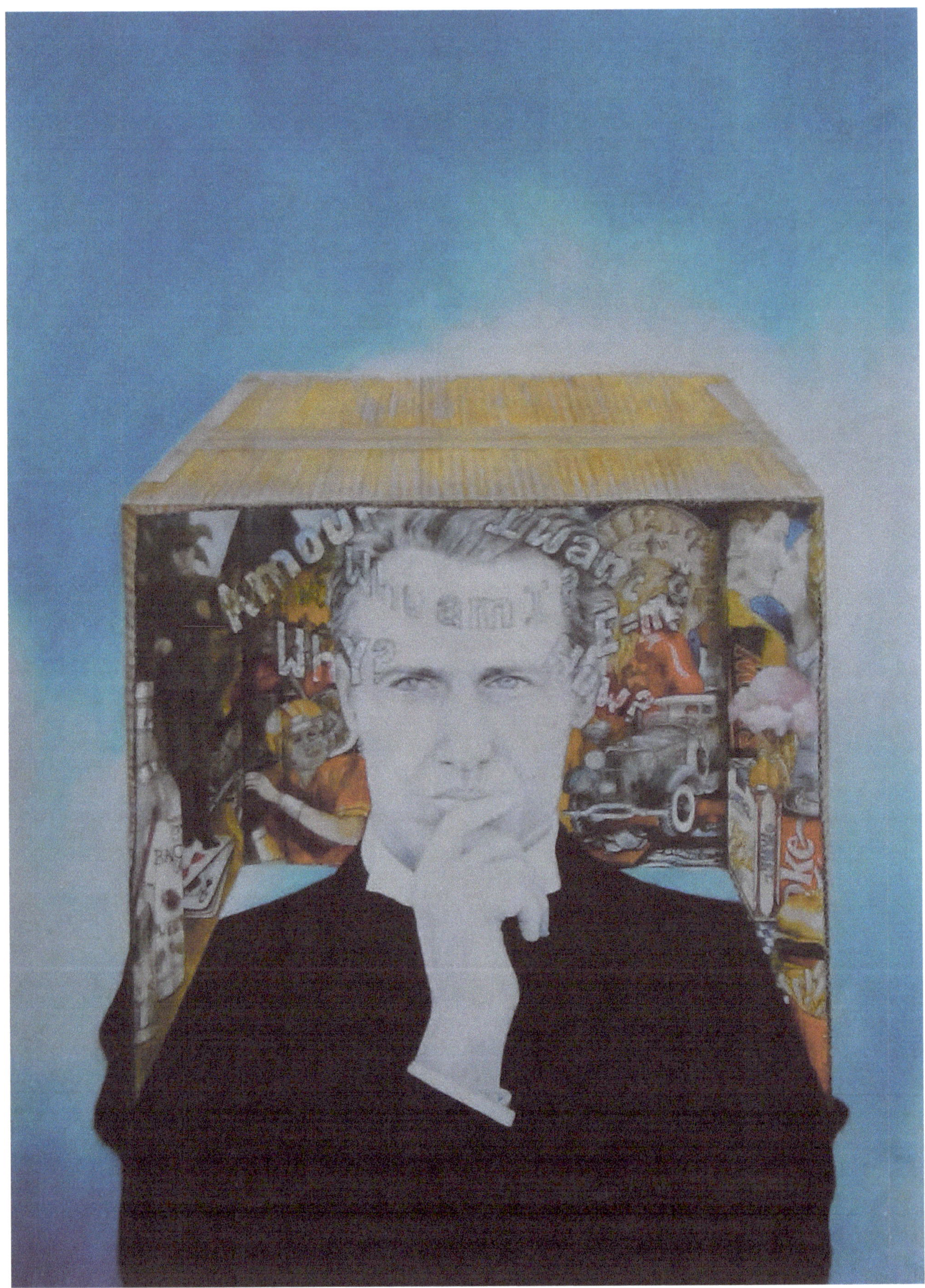

Illustration by Ginger Gilmour

WORDS

Words lost in translation
True meanings confused
Lead to misunderstandings
And even permanent feuds
Just one misplaced word
Can make things quite dark
So we need to be careful
When we speak from the heart
Promises made with good intentions
Can so easily be misconstrued
When those with a different agenda
Suddenly change all the rules
It's not always about being right
Or somebody's done you wrong
It's often about who has the front
To actually take you on
What you say without thinking
Can often cause so much pain
Sometimes it's just not enough
To simply say that you won't
Make that mistake again
They say that counting to ten
Is the best thing you can do
But that slight hesitation
Can make some people think
That what you eventually say
Isn't actually true
But then sometimes it don't matter
Whatever you say
There will always be someone
Who's already made their mind up
Anyway!

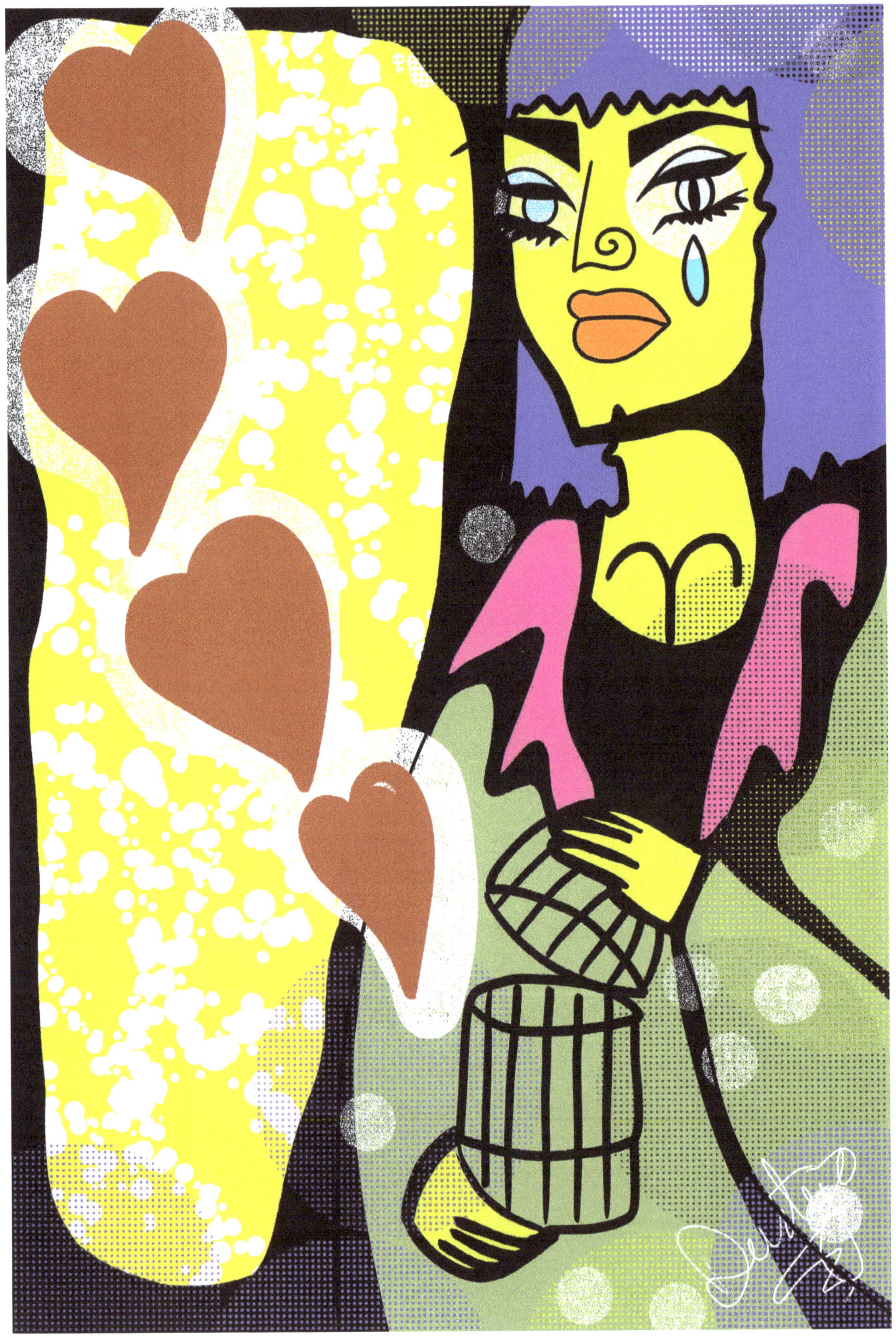

Illustration by Dusty O.

WHEN I SAID

When I told you I loved you
It came from my heart
When you sinned I forgave you
Kept you warm in the dark
I tried so very hard
To be honest with you
But you chose to lie
And treat me like a fool
But despite what you've done
And all the things that you've said
I still haven't stopped loving you
Stopped loving you yet
They say time is a healer
And that I'll make it through
But as yet nobody's
Been able to tell me
How long it's gonna take me
Before I can stop loving you

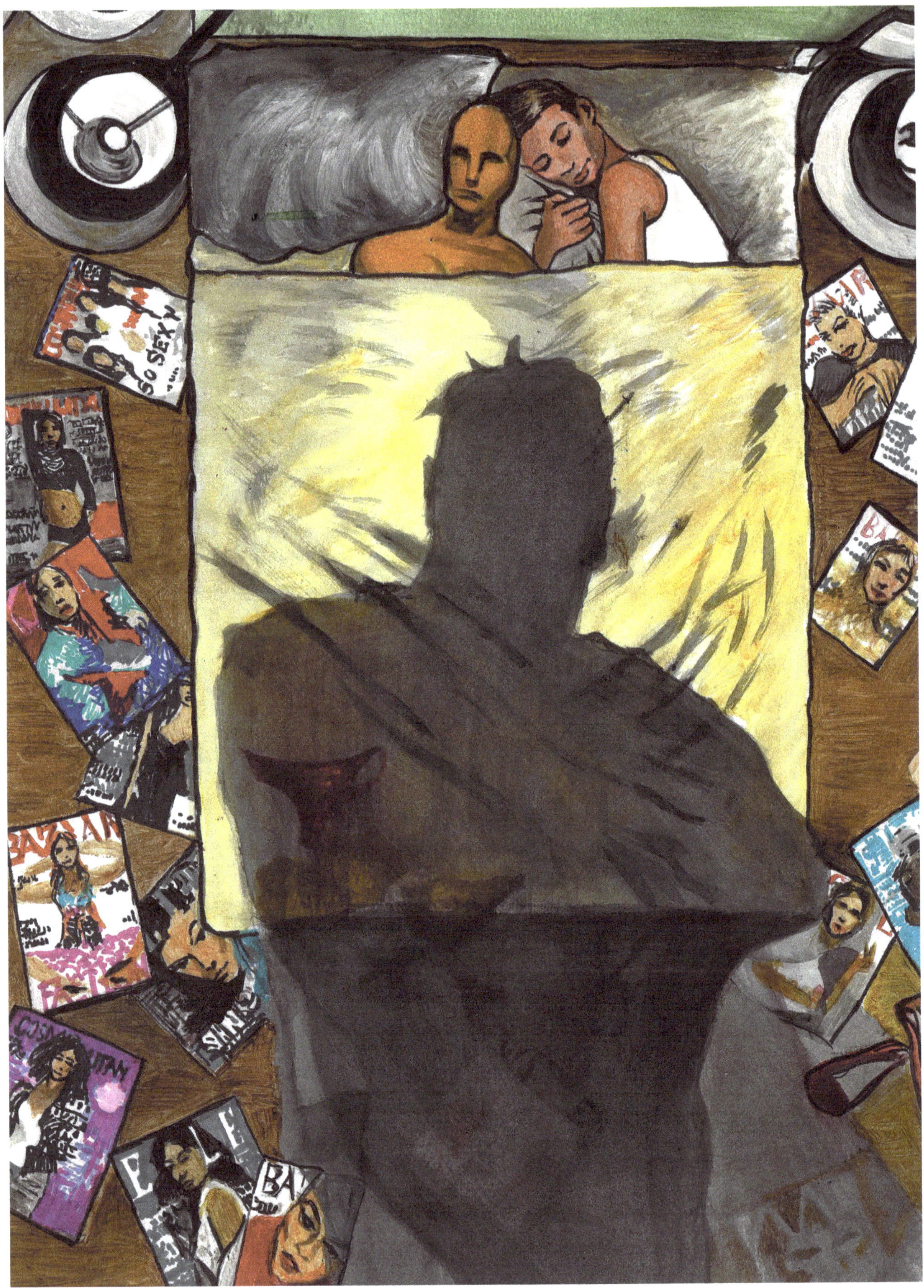

Illustration by Howard Priestley

THE GIRL ON THE QUARTER TO EIGHT

She lays down with strangers
Night after night
Dances with shadows
Exposed by the moon's light
Paperback heroes
Come to life in her bed
Knights on white horses
Fight for her honour inside her head
Stardom is coming
It's just a matter of time
No doubt about it
She's next in line
Hollywood beckons
They're all on the phone
It's anyone's guess
How far she will go
She's wrapped round a lover
On a white sandy beach
Clutching her Oscar
Making a speech
She steps out of a limo
And the cameras go wild
She's on the cover of Vogue
This year's icon of style
She has lunch at the Ivy
Takes tea at the Ritz
Has dinner at Nubo
With Tom Cruise and Brad Pitt
Takes the red eye to New York
With Naomi and Kate
Has cocaine for breakfast
Just to keep her awake
Hitting the catwalk
In a Karl Lagerfeld gown
In front of Jay-Z and Beyoncé
And an A list Hollywood crowd
Then with a shudder and shake
A screeching of brakes
Her train finally comes to halt
At a quarter to eight
And until she's finished her shift
On the checkout in Tesco
Stardom will just have to wait

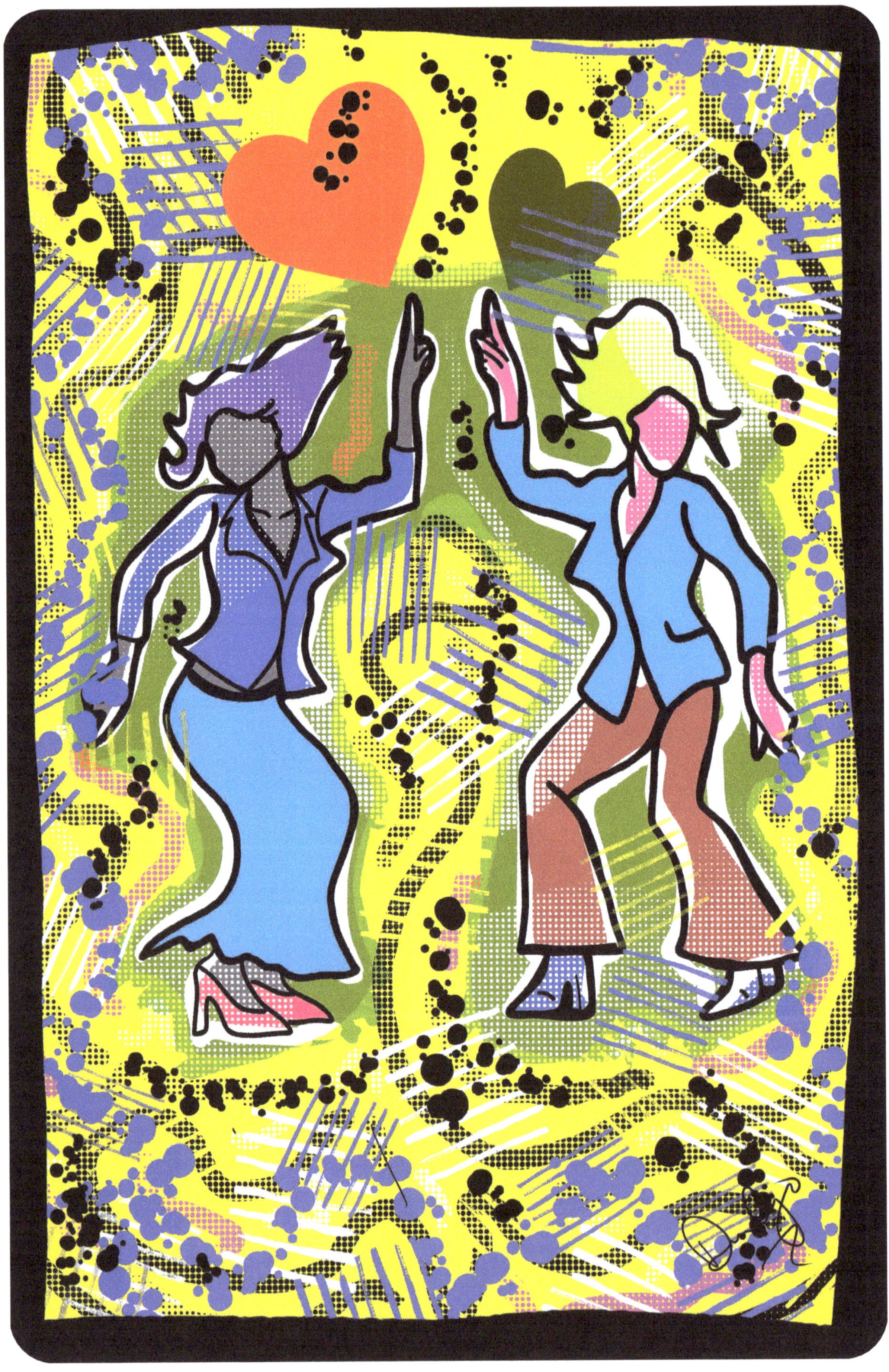

Illustration by Dusty O.

LAST NIGHT AT THE DISCO

Sophie Ellis-Bextor threatened murder on the dance floor
Rod Stewart claimed that Maggie May had kicked him in the head
The Rolling Stones complained they couldn't get no satisfaction
Then Chris de Burgh started banging on about some women dressed in red
Madonna tried to tell us that she was like a virgin
Before George Michael suddenly announced that he would never dance again
The Eagles said that they were just about to check into the Hotel California
And they'd decided to leave Prince outside standing in the purple rain
Tiny Tim said he was going to tiptoe through the tulips
Mick Hucknull said so what, I've just fallen from the stars
The Police then said that's nothing, we're walking on the moon
David Bowie reckoned he was actually a spider visiting from Mars
The Weather Girls said omg it's started raining men
And Michael Jackson told us that his best friend was a rat called Ben
Saint Bobby Geldof asked us tell me why I don't like Mondays
And the Bangles butted in and said but Mondays are our fun days
Sir Elton John said hold the front page news I'm still standing
Then ABC said someone's shot me with a poison arrow straight through the heart
And Platters started to complain that smoke was getting in their eyes
Then R Kelly stopped us in our tracks and said I believe I can fly
And Doctor and the Medics said ok take me up to the spirit in the sky
Chris Rea said that he was driving home for Christmas
Then Mariah Carey pointed out that it was only the fourth of July
The DJ then killed the dance floor by playing Kylie's I should be so lucky
And that's when everyone decided it was time to call it a night

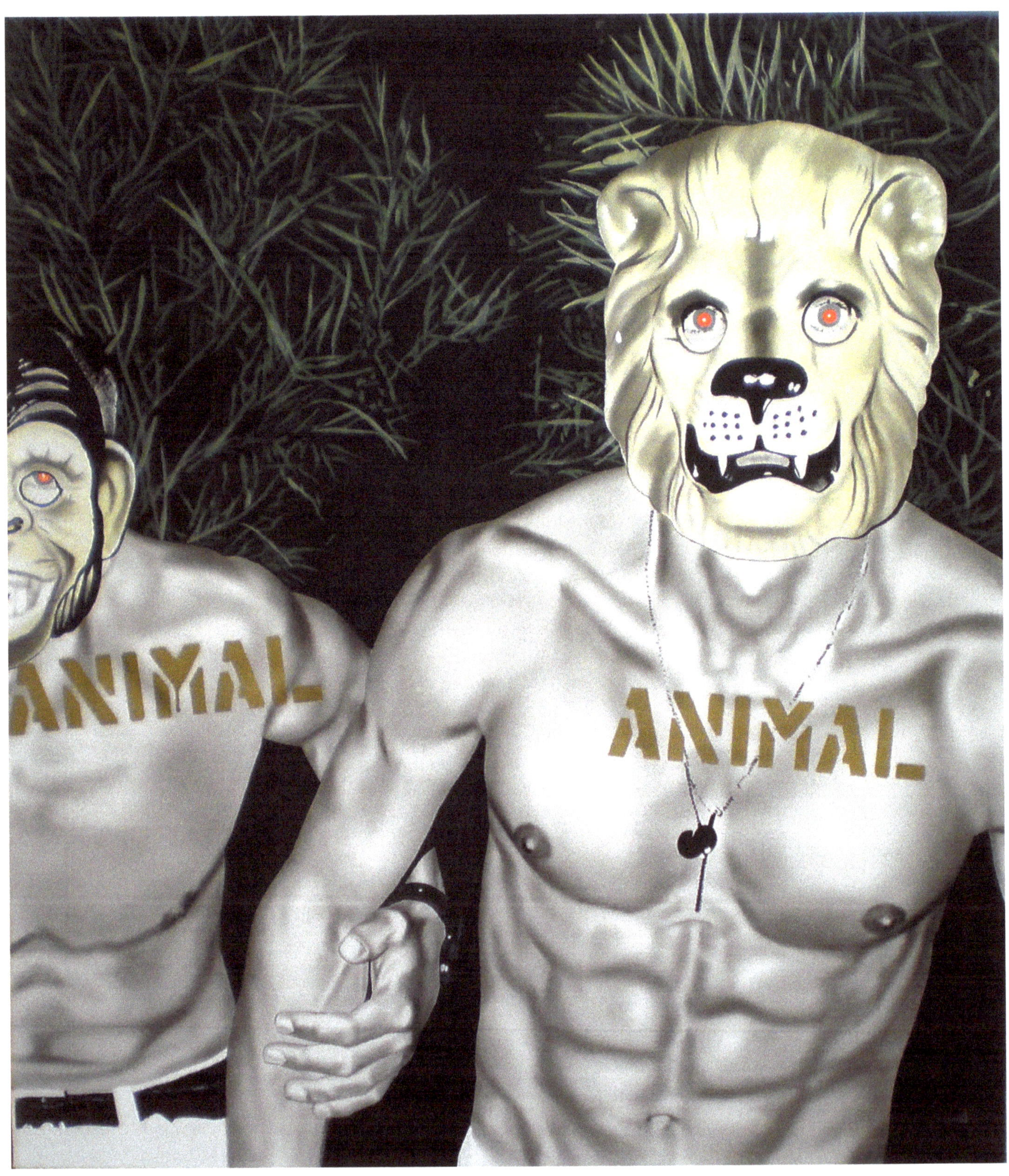

Illustration by Mark Wardel AKA TradeMark

THE DARK SIDE OF LIFE

There's a dark side of life where people engage
In consensual pleasures or so they claim
What goes on behind doors is anyone's guess
But those who turn up are all dressed to impress
Men head to toe in black leather, women in rubber and lace
All wearing one of those black Batman type masks
In order to hide their face
Cars arrive after dark on a suburban side street
And curtains start twitching as neighbours are having a peek
It's one those fancy dress parties, Roger tells Mavis his wife
Well why are they all dressed exactly the same then she says
Something just doesn't seem right
I'm going to call the police this just doesn't look right to me
They're obviously up to no good dressed like that it's obscene
You shouldn't do that love he said
Wearing black's not a criminal offence
You seem to forget something Roger
I'm chair of Neighbourhood Watch
So I'm duty bound to report anything out of the ordinary
And this sort of thing needs to stop
And if they're not doing anything wrong
Then they won't mind explaining what's going on to the cops, will they Roger?
Omg what on earth is he wearing
Roger quickly you've got to see this
He's in one of those gimpy outfits
And she's barely covering her bits
Roger hand me the phone they've left me with no other option
I've got to put a stop to this now
Didn't I tell you there was something
About that woman
I said there was something about her that I didn't like
What kind of people dress up like that
Perverts do Roger, perverts, I told you that woman weren't right
And I've been proved right again haven't I Roger
God only knows what's going on in that house tonight
A fancy dress party in Pinner on a Wednesday night indeed
Just hand over the phone now I'm definitely going to call the police
A fancy dress party Roger, how could you be so naïve?

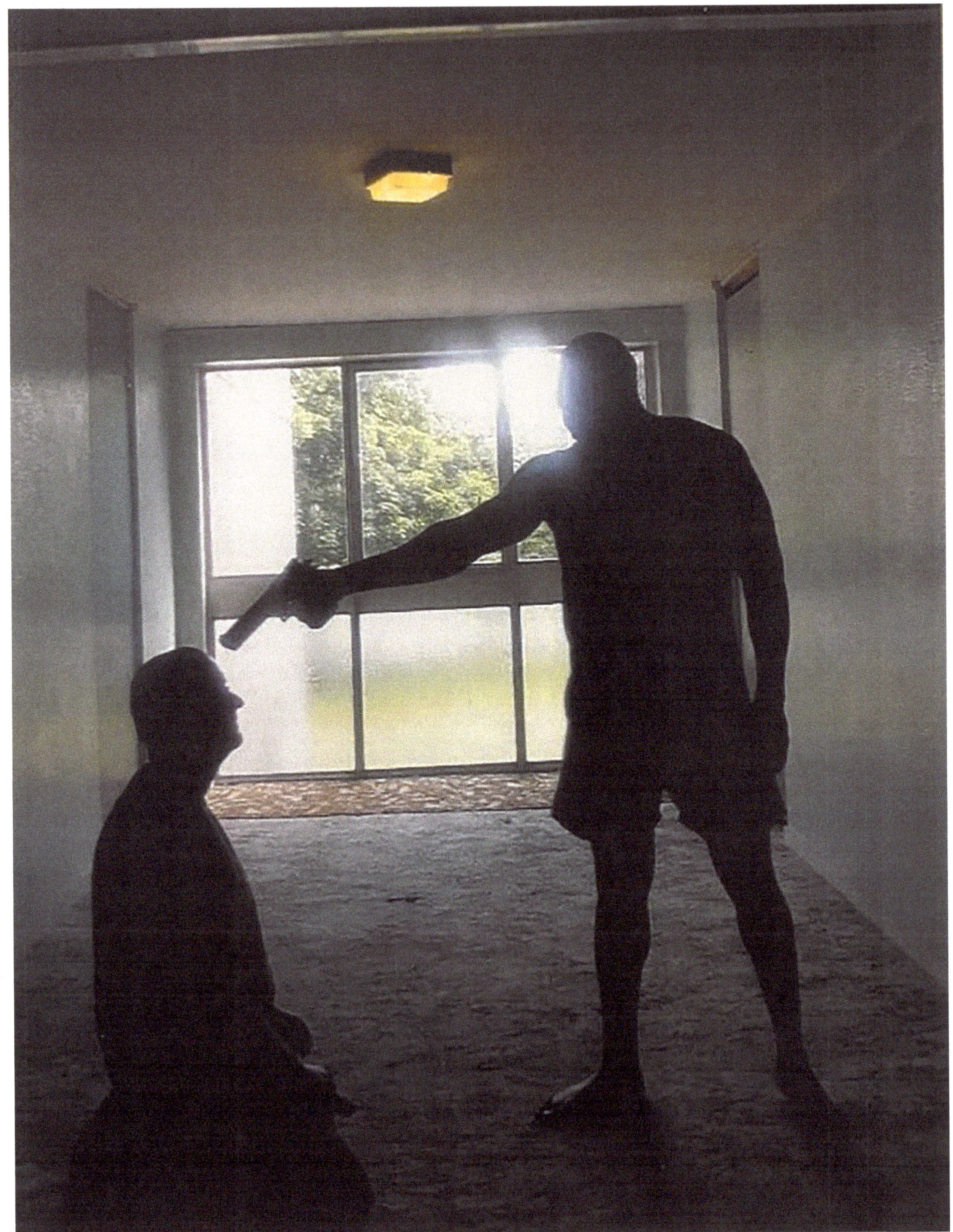

Illustration by Gerald O Dowd

SOLDIER OF FORTUNE

He's a soldier of fortune
A man with no heart
He lives in the shadows
And works in the dark
He's just a paid killer
To him it's merely a job
He'll kill men, women and children
He'll even shoot the pet dog
If things start to go wrong
He will simply change sides
It's not about honour
Or even a matter of pride
He will take everyone out
Leave no witness behind
He just gets the job done
He's a killer for hire
If a comrade is wounded
They will just end up dead
But he won't waste his bullets
He'll just cut their throats instead
Rape is part of his MO
It's merely the spoils of war
They're going to get killed anyway
He's just having some fun before
He's a professional killer
He doesn't observe the law
The Geneva Convention
Means nothing to him
There are no rules in his wars

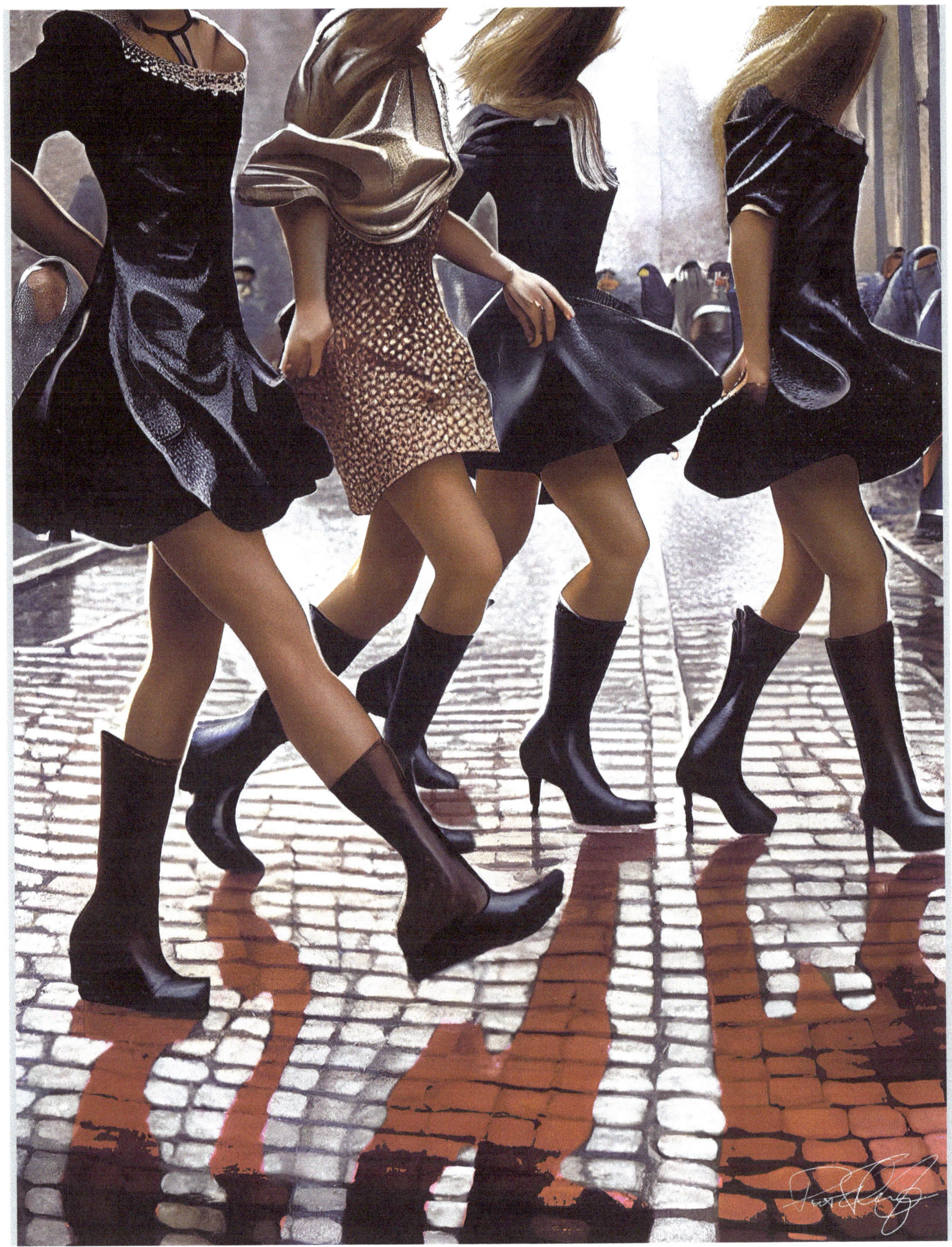

Illustration by Pat Flanagan

NIGHT CHILDREN

See the night time children
Stepping on the beat
Daddy's little angels
Dressed to kill
Turning up the heat
They head towards the neon lights
Lighting up a different world
As the new age hippies
Begin to scream out loud
Have you heard the word
Have you heard the word
As the city suits
Start heading home
The children from suburbia
Begin to hit the streets
Groups of teenage girls
Barely out of school
Help each other paint their faces
As they try to look real cool
The boys turn up
In twos and threes
Begin to strut their stuff
As they swagger past
The groups of girls
Trying to catch their eye
The queues outside the clubs
Begin to grow in size
As nervous girls approach
Flash their fake IDs
And disappear inside

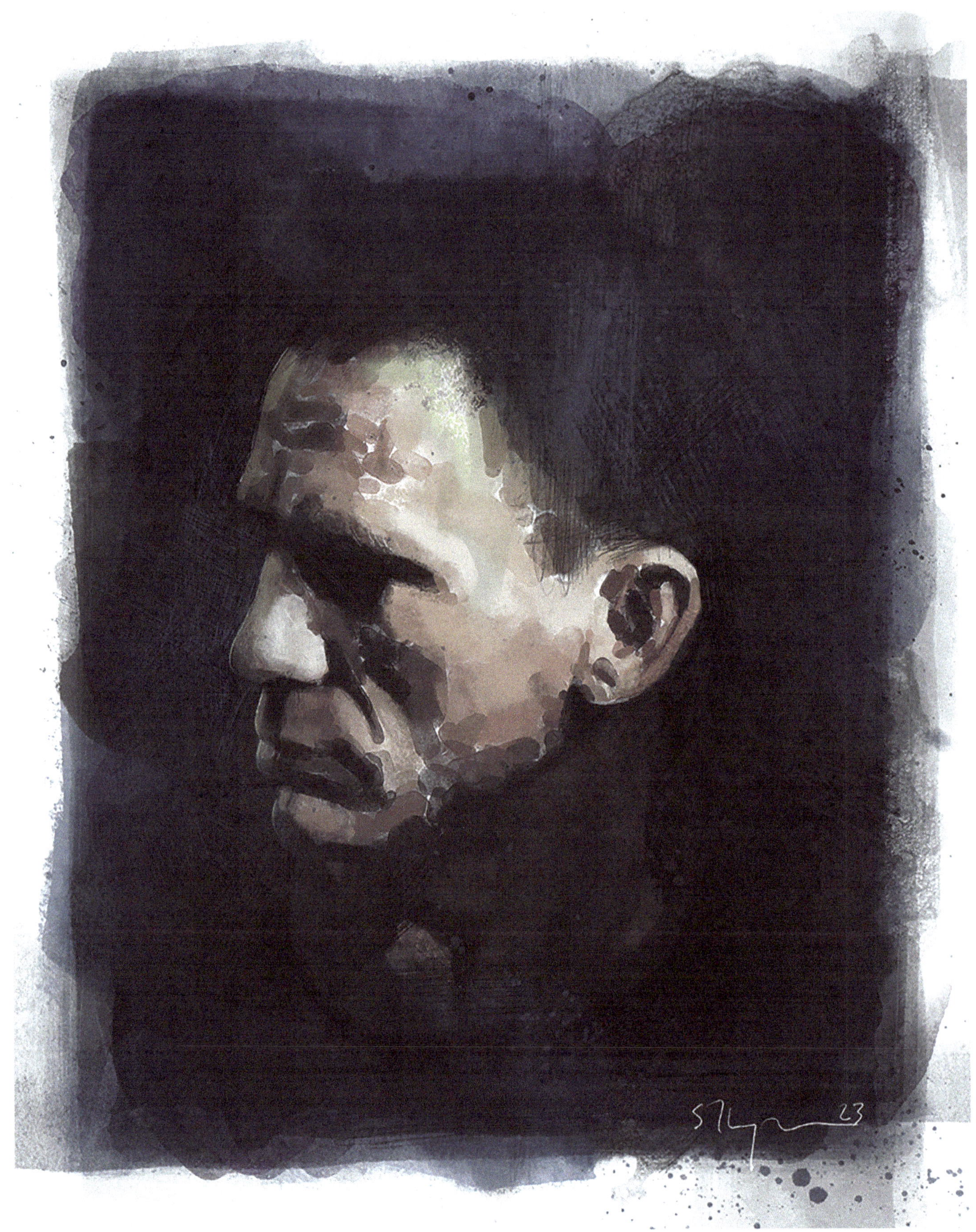

Illustration by Simon Thompson

PEEL BACK THE SKIN

Peel back the skin
See the carnage within
Nobody's perfect
We all have our sins
Is lust a curse
Or just part of life
Some people's pleasure
Needs a little more spice
For some lying and cheating
Is a way of life
Some men who will tell you
They need more than one wife
They just can't resist
Taking things further
Thinking what she doesn't know
Ain't gonna hurt her
For some it's a dream
A fantasy thing
And they manage to keep
Lust and desires locked within
For others it's more about ego
The chase is just part of the game
They develop their powers of
seduction
By doing it over and over again
For some being loved
Is just not enough
They rely on their charm
And basically bluff
They say the right things
At the right time
And once the hook's set
They reel in the line
Peel back the skin
See the carnage within
Nobody's perfect
We all have our sins

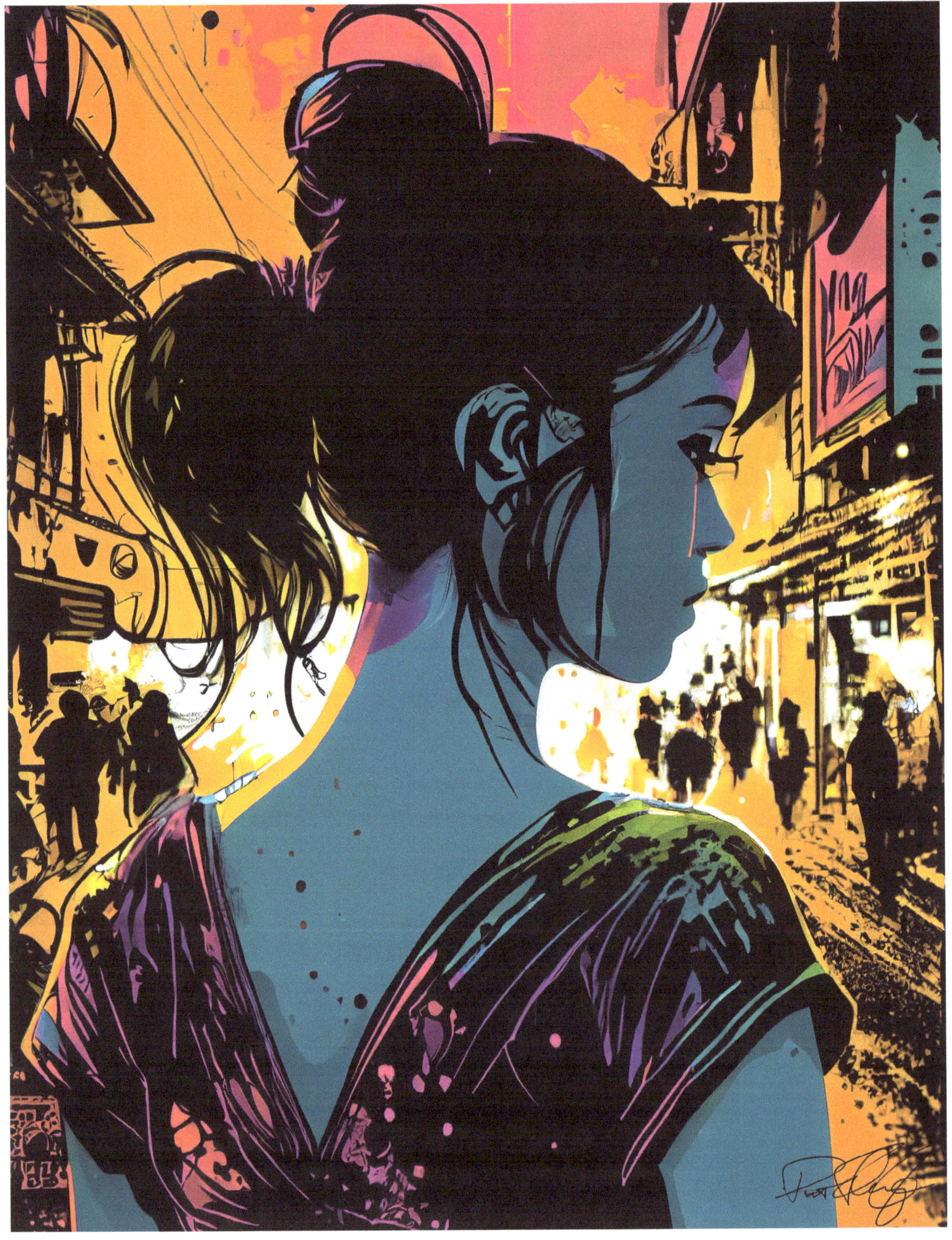

Illustration by Pat Flanagan

THE GIRL FROM NAGASAKI

The girl from Nagasaki
Rode the bullet train
Ended up in Tokyo
Never went home again
The girl from Nagasaki
Rode the bullet train
Ended up in Tokyo
A city full of pain
Rich men come to hang out
At night with their friends
In nightclubs full of pretty girls
Who entertain old men
Sex is never mentioned
Everyone's discreet
The girls are merely company
They're here to meet and greet
Girls flock to the city
To escape their rural life
Hoping to meet rich men
And become devoted wives
Tokyo's the place to be
According to their friends
A girl can have her pick
It's full of rich and lonely men
But life in Tokyo
Ain't so fast and free
It's full of danger and intrigue
That will strip away your dignity
You'll have to work your ticket
Your time don't last that long
Before you're on the streets
Turning tricks to eat
The girl from Nagasaki
Rode the bullet train
Ended up in Tokyo
And never went home again

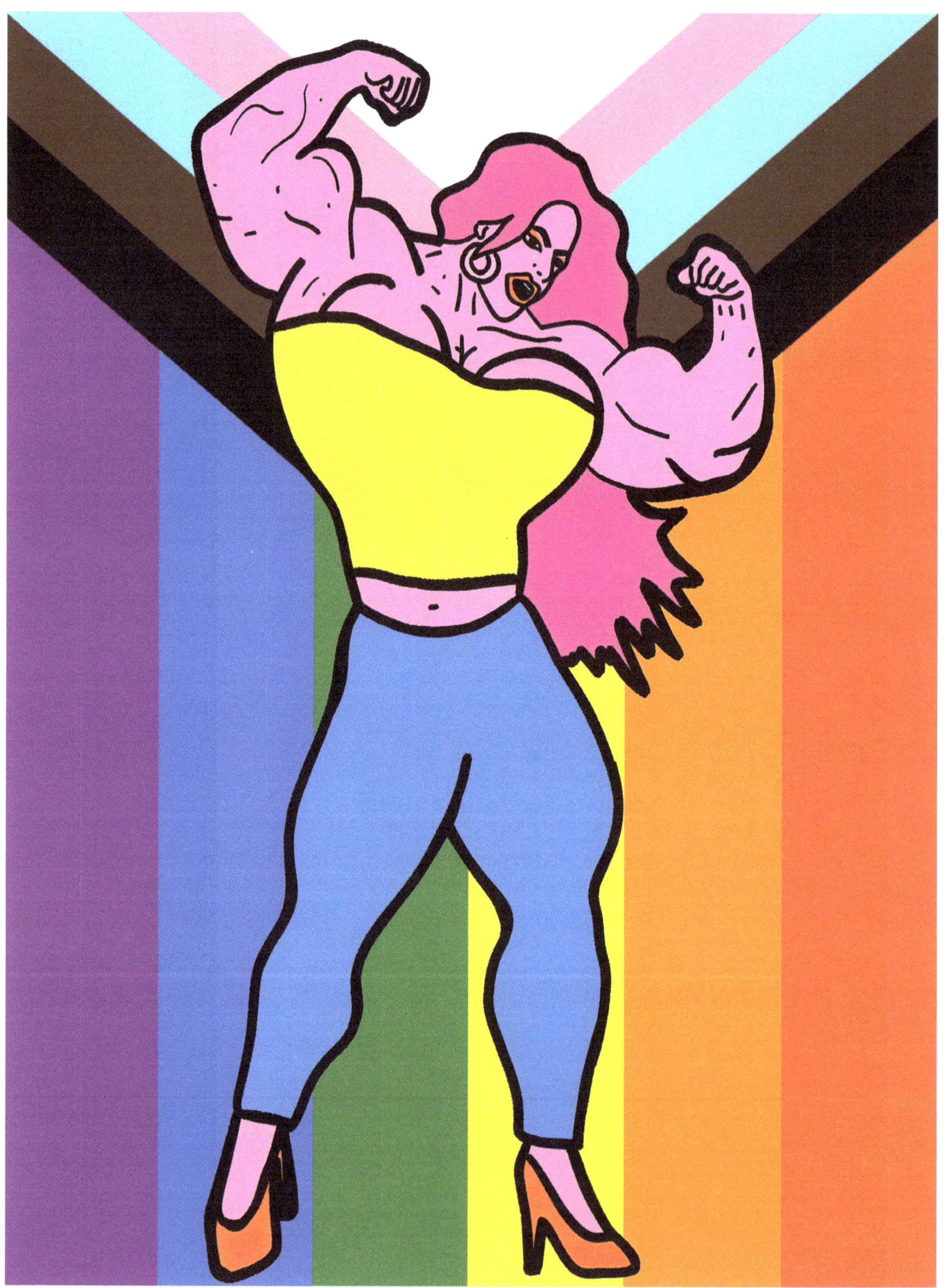

Illustration by Dusty O.

BABY DOES

Baby's full of promises
Baby's full of woe
But even when she makes you cry
She's the girl you wanna know
Baby's full of indecision
She likes to question why
Baby's got her own agenda
And it ain't the same as mine
Baby's got her own plans
She's got things to do
If you ain't on the same page
She'll just cut you loose
Baby doesn't care
Well that's what Baby says
But then Baby calls me back
When I turn to walk away
Baby's got a headache
Baby isn't in the mood
Baby wants to be alone
You'll have to leave the room
Baby's really busy
Baby doesn't have the time
She'll call back when she's ready
Leave you hanging on the line
Baby will and Baby won't
Baby does and Baby don't
Baby's indecisive
Baby keeps me running blind
Baby knows what Baby wants
But then she'll change her mind
Baby's got a wish
To blow me away
Then she goes and smiles
And I beg for her to stay

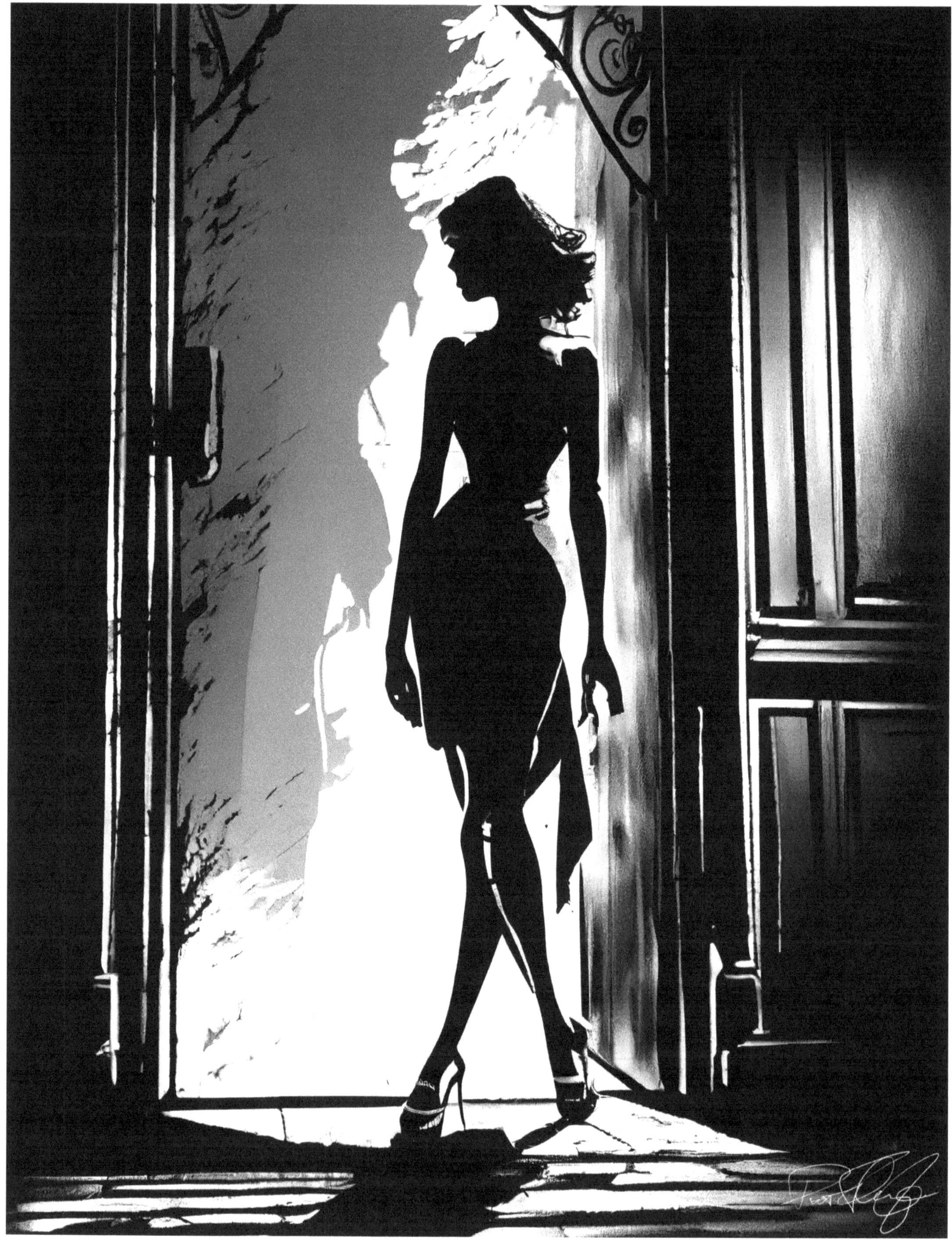

Illustration by Pat Flanagan

SHE WAS AND SHE IS

She's a vision of beauty
All dressed in black
A woman of virtue
Well I wouldn't say that
She'll wiggle her hips
And with a wink of an eye
She'll blow you away
With a cynical smile
She knows you'll be looking
And she's looking too
She's already worked out
Your every move
You'll go in for the kill
She'll just wave you away
Tell you to come back and try
When you're ready to play
She'll throw you a line
And then let it go
You'll dance to her tune
Before you even know
She'll call it on
Then tell you to leave
Blow you away
Like a leaf in the breeze
She'll make her move
Come straight on to you
Before spinning around
And leaving the room
She loves playing games
She'll mess with your head
She'll make you believe
She wants you in her bed
She was and she is
The girl of your dreams
She's every heroine
Villain and vamp
That you've ever seen
On the silver screen

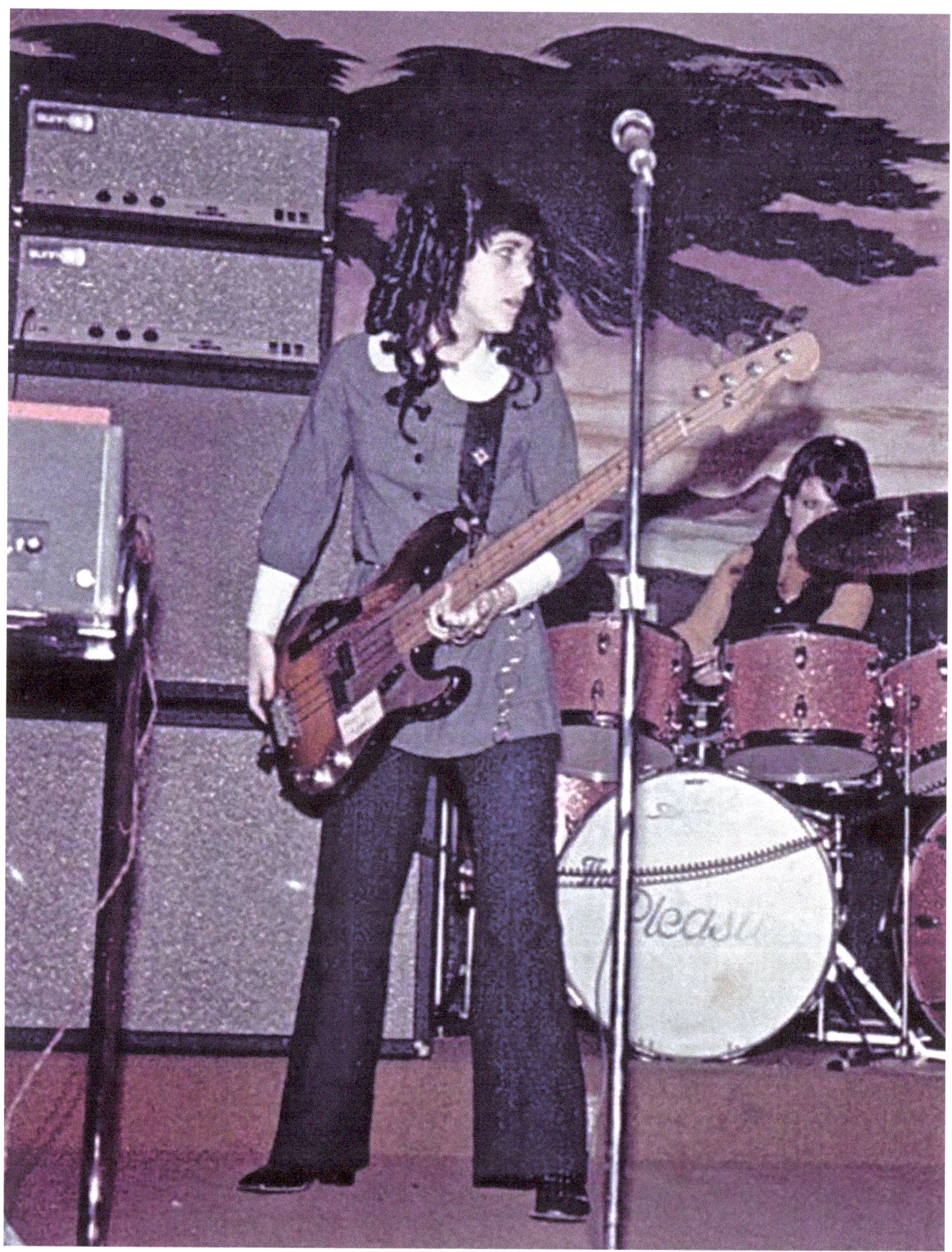

Illustration by Suzi Quatro

MEMPHIS BOUND

She's heading for Memphis
With a head full of dreams
A battered guitar case
One pair of jeans
Her grandfather's kit bag
Carries all that she owns
Heading into a world
That she's never known
Just a small town girl
With big ideas
She's going to make it
That much is clear
She's been listening to stories
Since she was a child
About her grandmother's
Once glamorous life
She's been playing for nickels
On her battered guitar
Saving up for a ticket
In an old whisky jar
Playing her songs
To a cow and a pig
On a stage made of hay
Now she's ready to gig
She's had no time for boys
They come sniffing around
They asked for a date
They've all been turned down
She's been too busy writing
Her book full of songs
Counting the days
Until she can finally move on
She's heading for Memphis
Chasing her dreams
She'll stand centre stage
And acknowledge the screams
She'll strum her guitar
To the roll of the drums
Then lift the roof off
With her first number one
Another small town girl
With a head full of dreams
She's counting the days
Until she's finally free

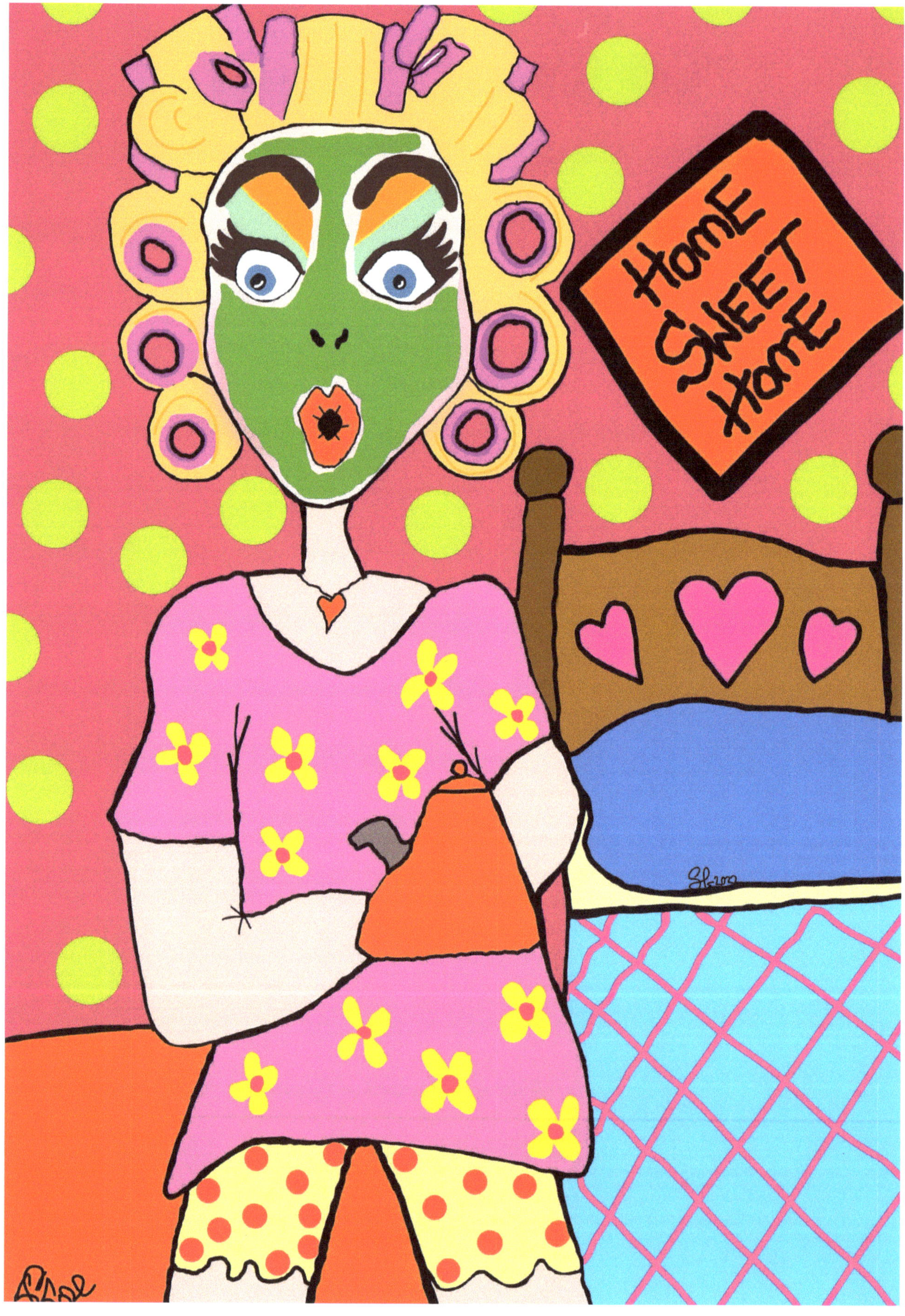

Illustration by Shaun George

ME AND MY BIG MOUTH

It's already way past midnight
and I'm here all alone
Lying in this empty bed wondering
if she's ever coming home
I wrap my arms around her pillow
I can smell her on the sheets
I hear laughter from the street outside
As a single tear rolls down my cheek
The headlights from a passing car
send shadows dancing round the room
Then suddenly it's plunged back into darkness
as a cloud envelops the night moon
I want to tell her that I'm sorry,
I will admit that I'm to blame
But I've said that so many times before;
will she believe that I can change?
I said things I didn't mean to say
I let my anger get ahead of me again
Why do I always jump straight in
Instead of simply counting up to ten
She said she wasn't coming back
As she walked off in the morning rain
And I told myself once she calms down
She'll be back and things will be ok
I turn towards the bedside table;
the time is now almost ten to four
She's never been this late and as I begin to panic
I hear her key turn in the door
I turn on the bedside lamp
and sit up straight in bed
And wait for her to come into the bedroom
And tell her that I'm sorry,
I didn't mean the things I said
And she looks at me,
rolls her eyes and nods her head
Climbs into bed beside me a
nd whispers in my ear
We'll see how sorry you are in the morning then
she said
When you wake me up the in morning with my
breakfast
Coffee, buttered toast and two poached eggs
And you'll be taking me out shopping in the
afternoon as well
And don't forget your credit card because you'll
need it for my new little black dress
And then I really started panicking
as I suddenly remembered
That I'd made myself an omelette
and used up all the bloody eggs
As I lay there wondering what I was going to do
I had a genius idea
Panic over,
I would simply make her cheese on toast instead
Until that was I started panicking again
about the cost of the black dress
Me and my big mouth
I lay there thinking to myself
As I closed my eyes and said you bloody idiot
underneath my breath

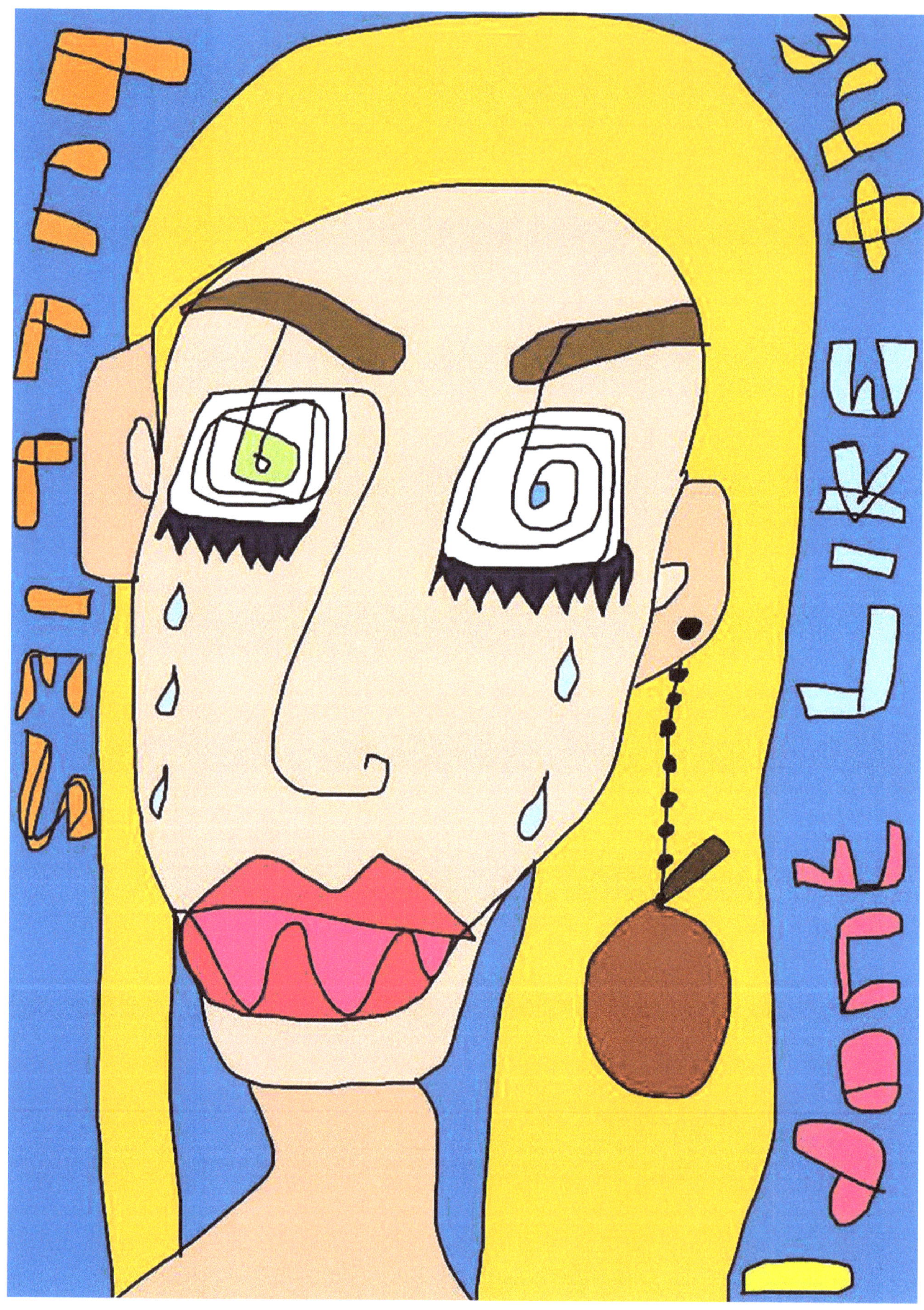

Illustration by Boy George

THE GIRL NEXT DOOR

I'm the girl next door
You don't remember me
The girl who used to smile at you
The one you pretended not to see
I'm the same little girl
That lived across the street
The girl who was in love with you
Who used to cry herself to sleep
I'm the girl you loved to torture
That girl you called names in the street
That awkward skinny little girl
The one you used to call that freak
You must remember Metal Micky
The girl with braces on her teeth
The one you used to entertain your friends
That girl you bullied, that was me
I'm the girl who had no friends
The girl that no one liked
The girl you used to bully
Who cried herself to sleep at night
I'm the girl next door
You must remember me
The girl you loved to torture
Every day for weeks
That awkward skinny little girl
Who lived across the street
I'm the ugly duckling
Who turned into a swan
The girl who was in love with you
But that love is now long gone
Yes I'm that very girl
The girl who struggled to belong
The girl who was in love with you
That love is now long gone

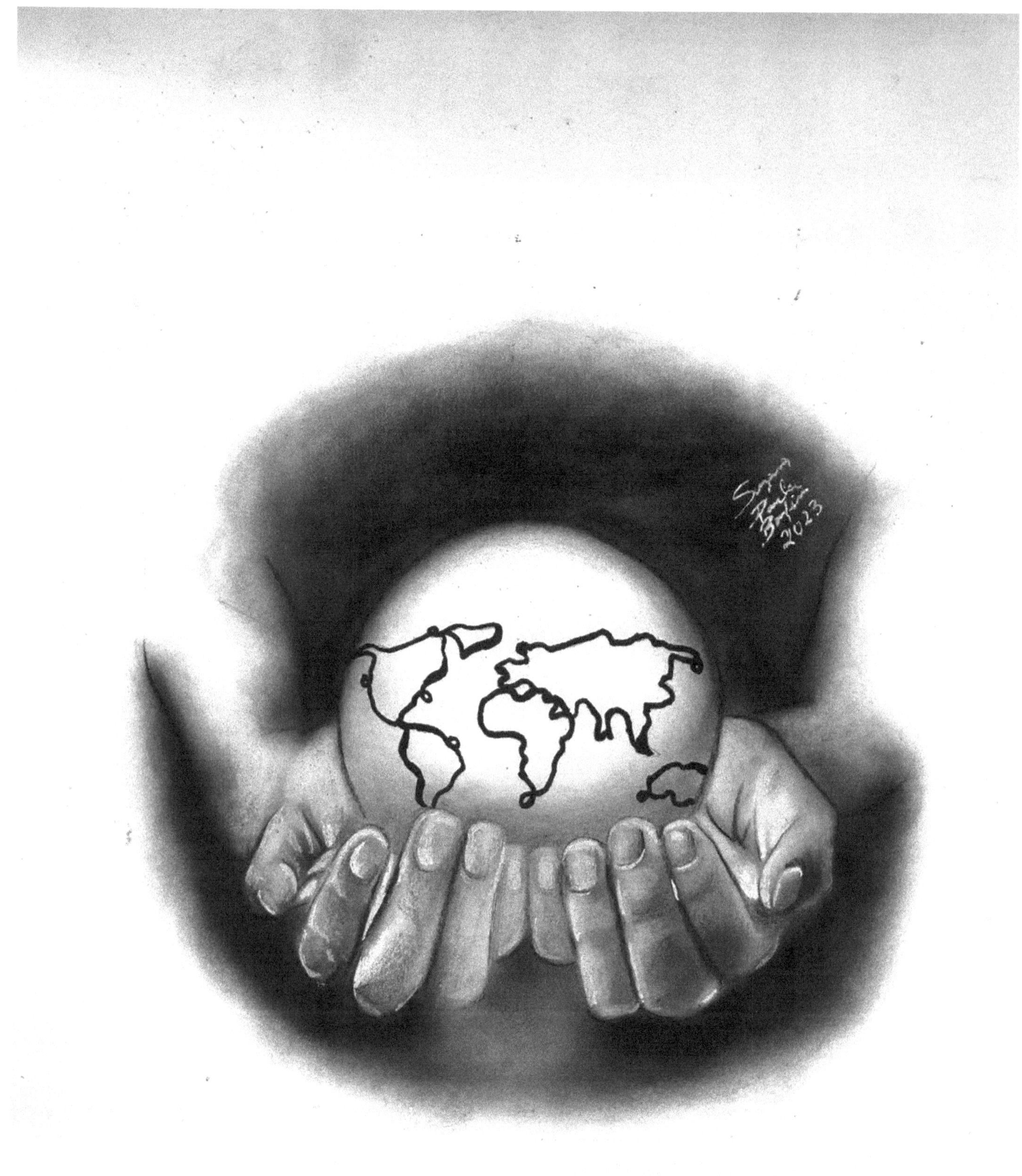

Illustration by Suzana Paula Bomfin

WHO DID THIS TO US?

Who took the sunshine
Out of the sky
Held back the rain
Let the rivers run dry
Who poisoned the air
That our children breathe
Who's behind this pandemic
This killer disease
Who did this to us
Who hates you and me
Who's stealing our future
The air that we breathe
How long have we got
How much time is left
Before the whole human race
Takes its last breath
Who's stolen the future
From all of our kids
Who's taken away
Their right to live
Where is your God
Who created mankind
In our hour of need
Has he left us behind
Who stole the love
The compassion and need
Who's cut Mother Earth
And is watching it bleed
Who took the sunshine
Out of the sky
Held back the rain
Let the rivers run dry
Who's poisoned the air
That our children breathe
Who's behind this pandemic
This killer disease

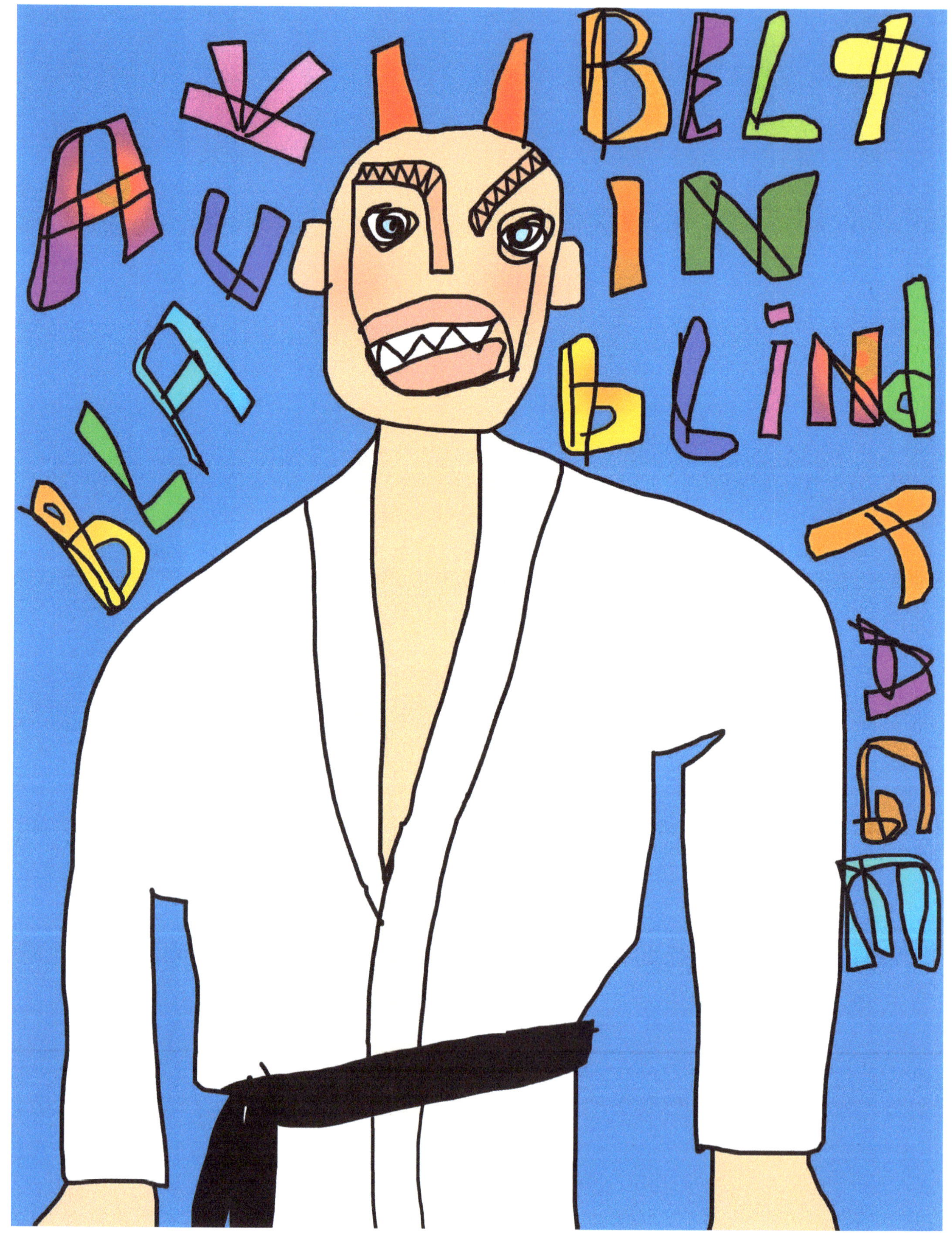

Illustration by Boy George

BORN OF YOUR FLESH

You were my hero
All I wanted to be
I looked up to you
But you never saw me
Born of your flesh
But you wouldn't know
Just how much your indifference
Was crushing my soul
You loved to talk about honour
You demanded respect
You made many mistakes
With no sign of regret
It was all about you
You were never wrong, always right
Your whole life was a gamble
Although money was tight
You berated our mother
Put the woman through hell
Portraying yourself as a good man
A part that you played so well
If your horse didn't win
Or you'd had a bad day
You'd vent your frustration and anger
By making your family pay
Despite your indifference
The fact you acted so dark
You were always my hero
Although you broke my heart
How you treated my mother
Is something I'll never forgive
You're the cause of most of my anger
You still affect the life that I live
Why didn't you notice
I was your flesh and bone
Such a compassionate man
With a heart made of stone

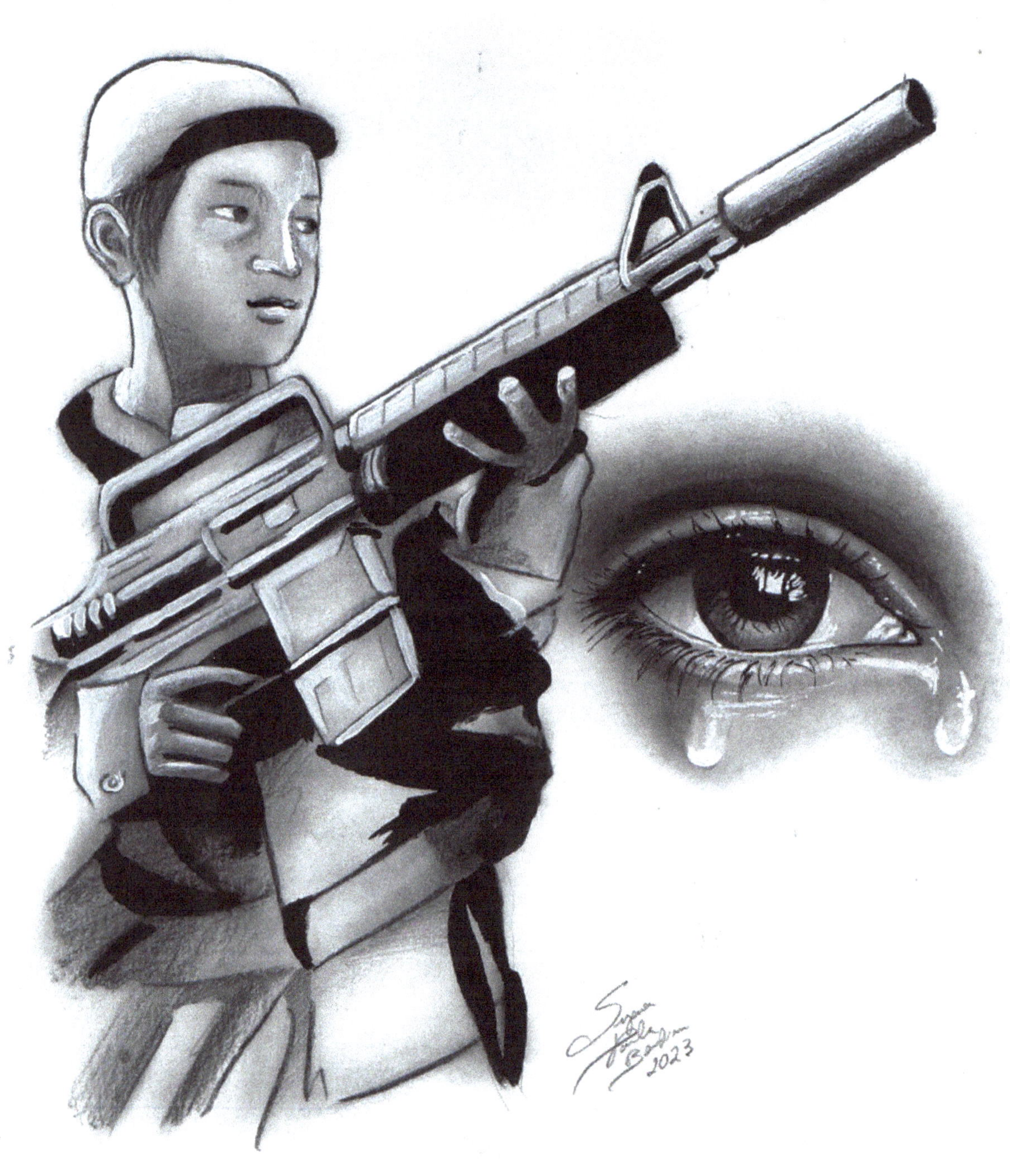

Illustration by Suzana Paula Bomfin

DEATH OF A CITY (Ukraine)

The city streets are empty, there's an air of sheer despair
Signs of life lay scattered on pavements, devastation everywhere
Pictures hanging on the wall fluttering in the wind
And somewhere in the rubble a mobile phone begins to ring
A fully laden table with food still on the plates
Is the only sign that family life had even taken place
An old lady shuffles past, her face etched with so much pain
As she searches for her husband who she will never see again
A dog sits by a bombed out building
Waiting for its master to come home
And once again the silence is shattered by a ringing mobile phone
The sirens start to scream again
As bombs rain down from the air
A mother hurries past with her daughter clutching onto a threadbare teddy bear
An ambulance screeches to a halt as men dig through the rubble with their hands
All in vain it seems, as they uncover yet another lifeless body of a man
These people are not soldiers, they don't carry bombs or guns
They're merely just collateral damage
They're just some other mothers' sons
Life has little value when it comes to war
Young men slaughtering one another
Without even knowing what they're fighting for

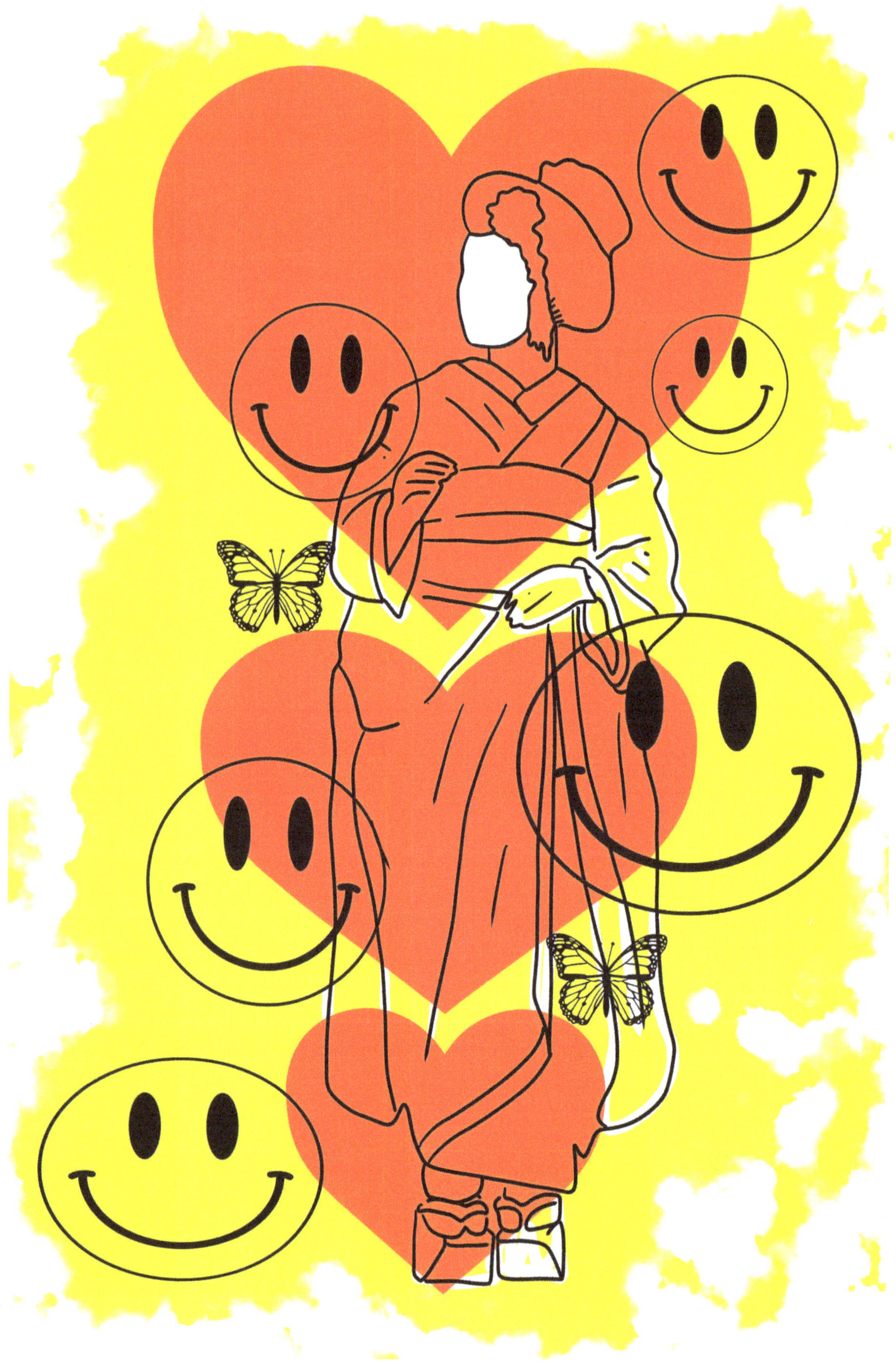

Illustration by Dusty O.

JAPANESE GIRLS

Born in Japan
Made in New York
She's a Japanese girl
No need to talk
Smiles with her eyes
Don't move her lips
She says it all
By wiggling those hips
Japanese girls
They're shy and demure
But they'll wreck your head
Behind closed doors
Japanese girls
Ain't what they seem
They'll take you places
Beyond your dreams
Japanese girls
Like porcelain dolls
You'll handle with care
Because you don't know
Peel back the layers
How far will you go
To uncover the truth
There are stories untold

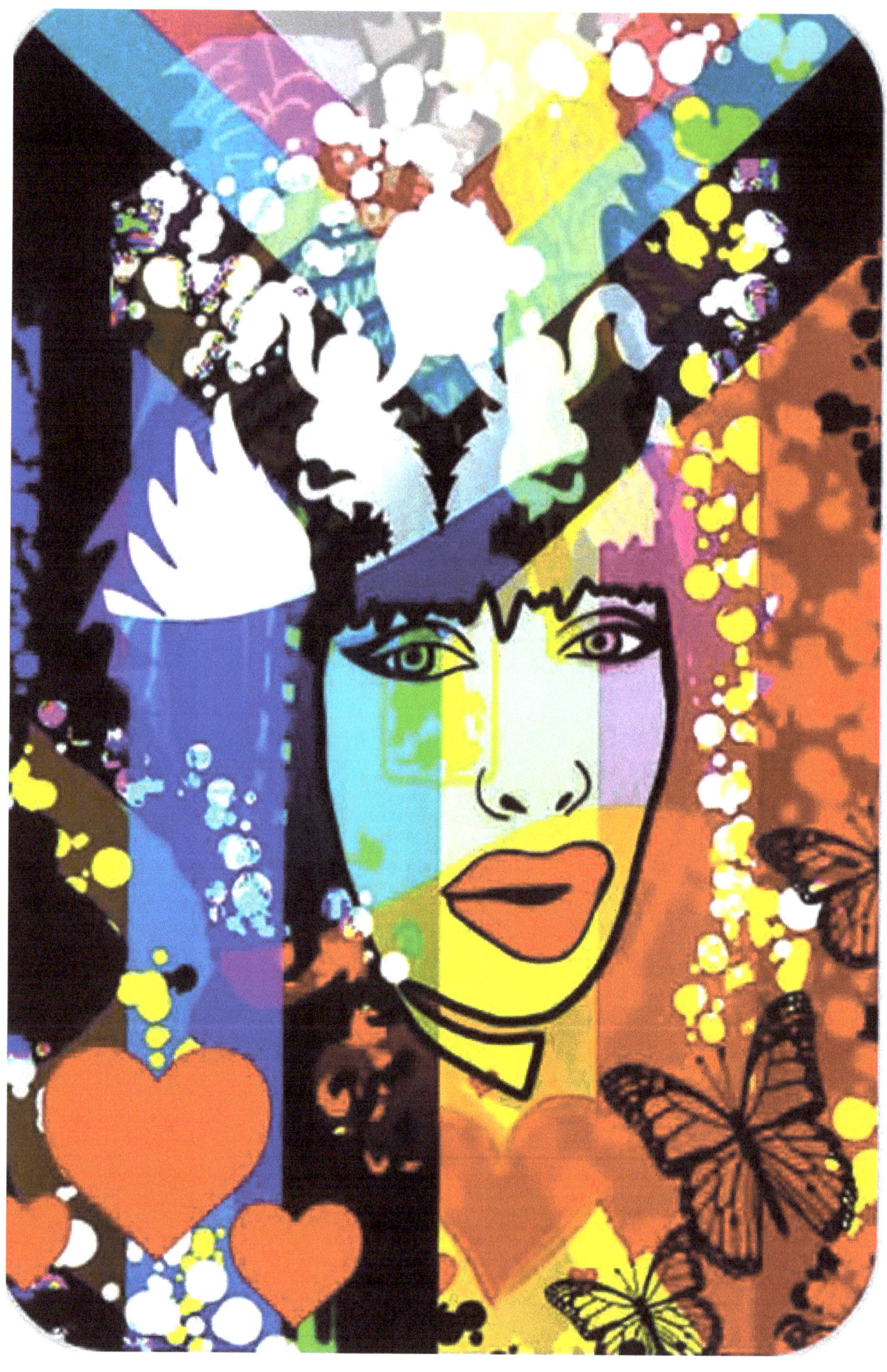

Illustration by Dusty O.

BORN THIS WAY

You're either born gay or not,
it's really as simple as that
It's not simply a case of you choosing
To change over to a different track
Whether you're a boy into boys
or you're a girl into girls
It's not simply a case of you choosing
To shave your head or put it into curls
You're born gay; it ain't a disease
It isn't something that can be cured
And putting someone through conversion therapy
Isn't something that anyone needs to endure
Gay men don't pose any threat to straight men
And exactly the same thing applies to the girls
In fact some people are born bisexual
And it's simply their personal choice where they choose to turn
A man kissing another man really shouldn't cause any alarm
How can showing somebody love be called a perversion?
And how can a public display of affection cause any kind of harm?
Gay people look exactly like you and me to be honest
You can't look at someone and tell that they're gay anyway
I was wearing makeup back in the 1980s as part of the New Romantics
And regularly dressed up like a peacock
and I can assure you I'm definitely straight
And I have several gay men and lesbian women
Who I consider to be my best mates

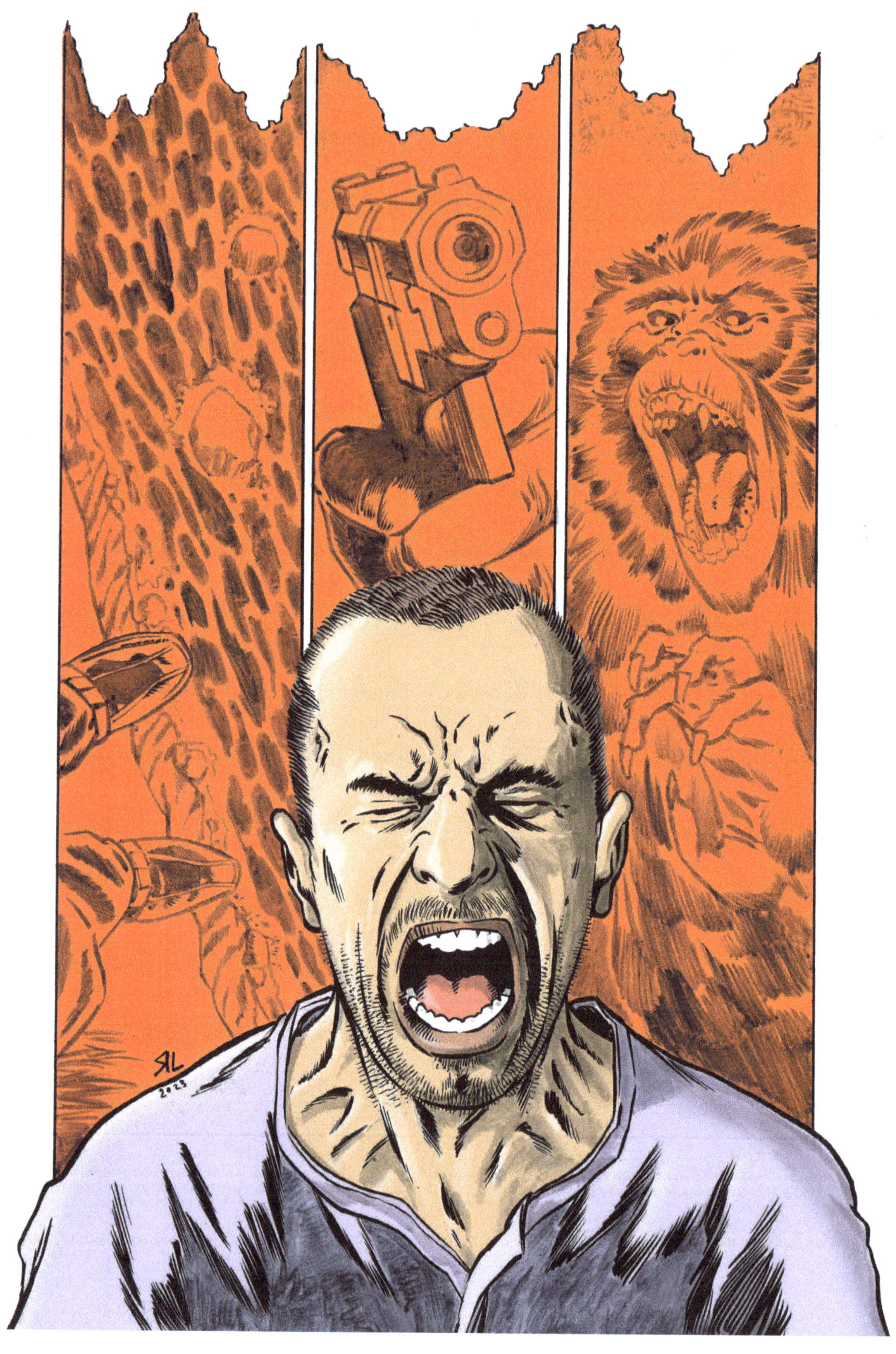

Illustration by Russ Leach

SCREAM

I feel like I'm drowning
This river runs deep
And I might lose my head
Before I get the chance to sleep
It feels like I'm standing
Too close to the edge
Someone's switched the dark on
And now I can't find my bed
I feel like a winner
But my destiny's a gun
I squeeze the trigger hard and wait
For a bang that never comes
I feel just like a stranger
On the wrong side of town
It's like someone's picked me up
While they've turned my world around
I feel like a junkie
There's a monkey on my back
So I'm waiting for the candy man
To help put me back on track
I feel like I've been here
A hundred times or more
I make it to the front of the queue
And then someone slams the door
I feel like I'm all alone
Even when I'm standing in a crowd
No one seems to want to talk to me
And yet the silence screams so loud
I just want to be the lover
I'm someone else's dreams
I want solitude, I want to be alone
I want to close my eyes and scream
Just want to close my eyes and SCREAM

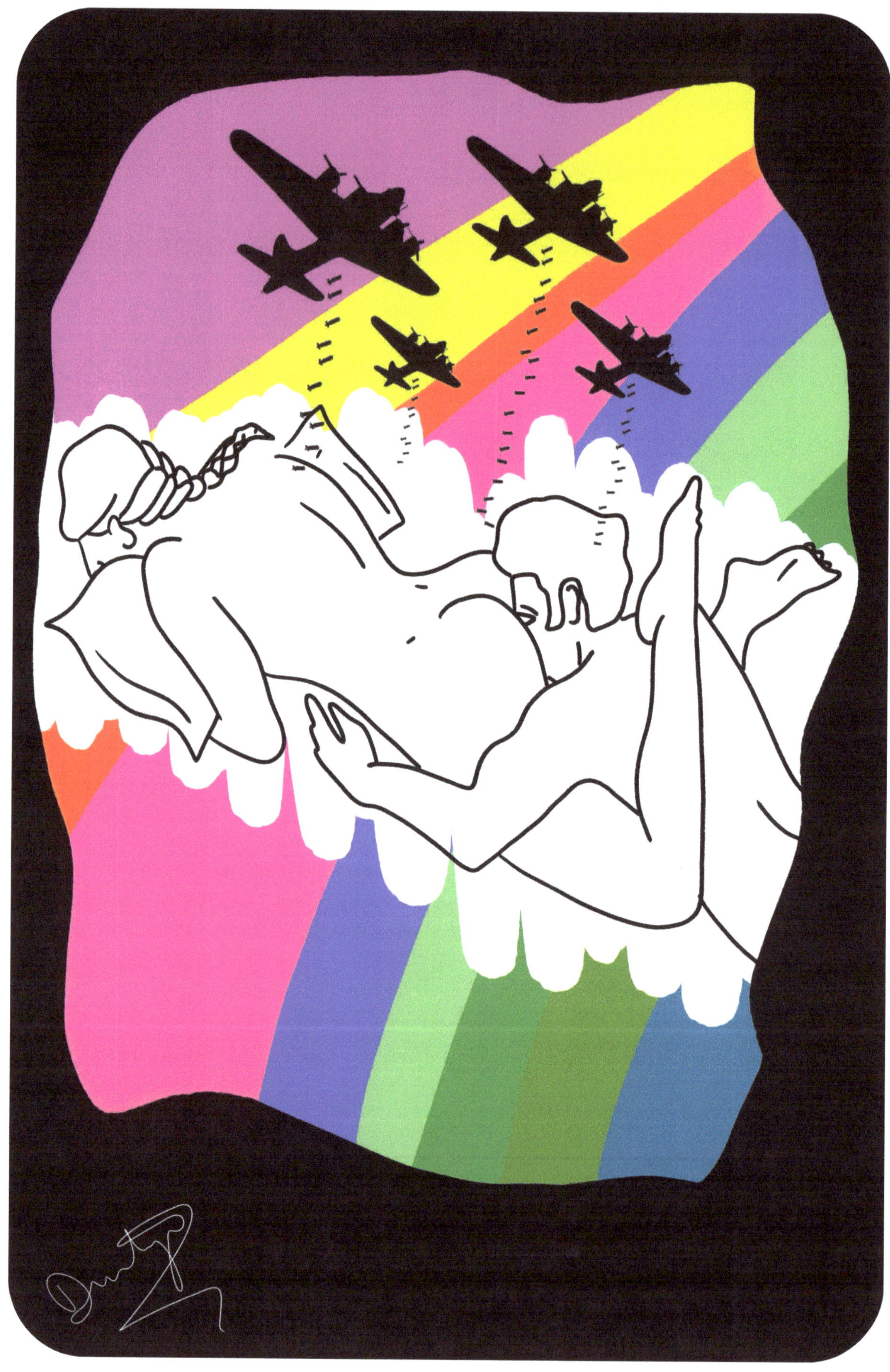

Illustration by Dusty O.

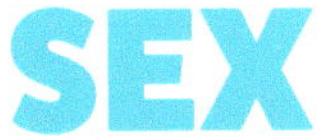

SEX

As you touch
And you caress
I breath heavily
And I sweat
I raise my head
You push me back
My muscles tense
Then I relax
You scream out loud
Grip my flesh
I feel your nails
Scrape down my chest
I begin to shiver
Start to shake
As I'm transported
To another place
You run your tongue
Across my face
You kiss me hard
Bite my lip
I feel your thighs
Begin to grip
You arch your back
Throw back your head
Pin my arms
Down to the bed
And I hear angels
Singing in my head
You take me places
In this bed
That ain't in any book
I've ever read
Do things with me
I've never done
Taken me to places
I've never dreamed I'd go

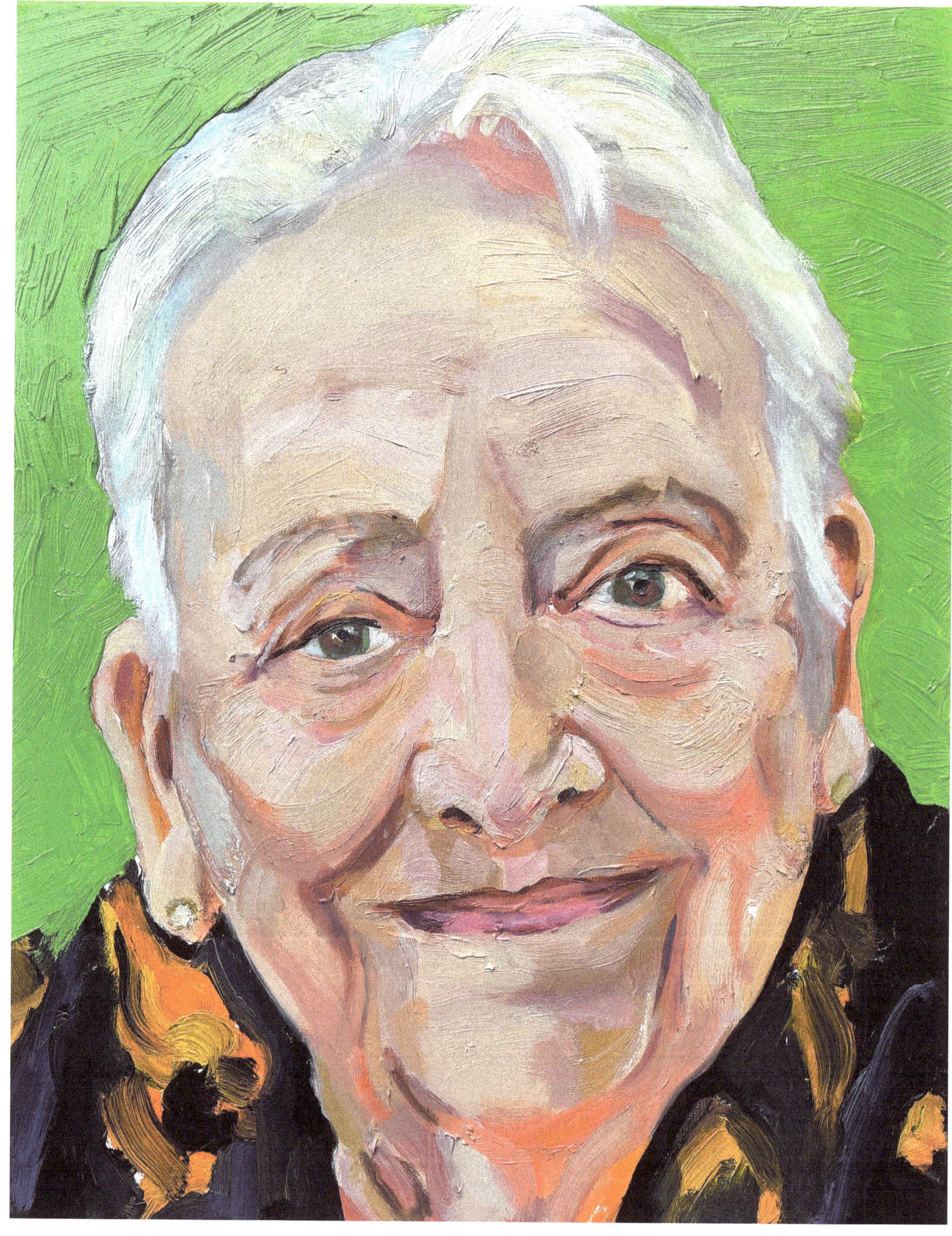

Illustration by JULIE BENNETT
You Always Knew Didn't You Mother 2021 Oil on canvas

THE LOVE OF A MOTHER

I am the product of a working class environment
My so-called formal education was provided by the state
I did however study human nature at the university of life
By virtue of the fact that I was born and raised on a post war social housing sink estate
Our parents raised six children in a tiny three bed end of terrace
Well when I say our parents, we were actually all raised by our mum
Although our father was around he otherwise preoccupied
With backing three legged horses that couldn't actually run
While our mother tended to her growing brood
Our father chased the next big win
Spending hours poring over all the form books and statistics in the Sporting Life
Only to end up pissing all his wages straight into the wind
To say that times were hard would be an understatement
Things just depended on whether or not our old man had a win
Friday nights were always full of tension and sometimes even fear
Waiting for him to come back home not knowing whether he'd be happy wasn't always clear
If he'd had a good day at the bookies it would be fantastic
Chocolate bars all round and often even fish and chips for tea
But if he'd blown his wages, which would often happen
We'd have beans on toast and then be sent to bed immediately
And although I can say with hand on heart that none of us went hungry
I had no idea that that was because our mother went without
In order to make sure that we always had something hot to eat
Which is why my mother is my hero
The only person on this earth who has always loved me unconditionally

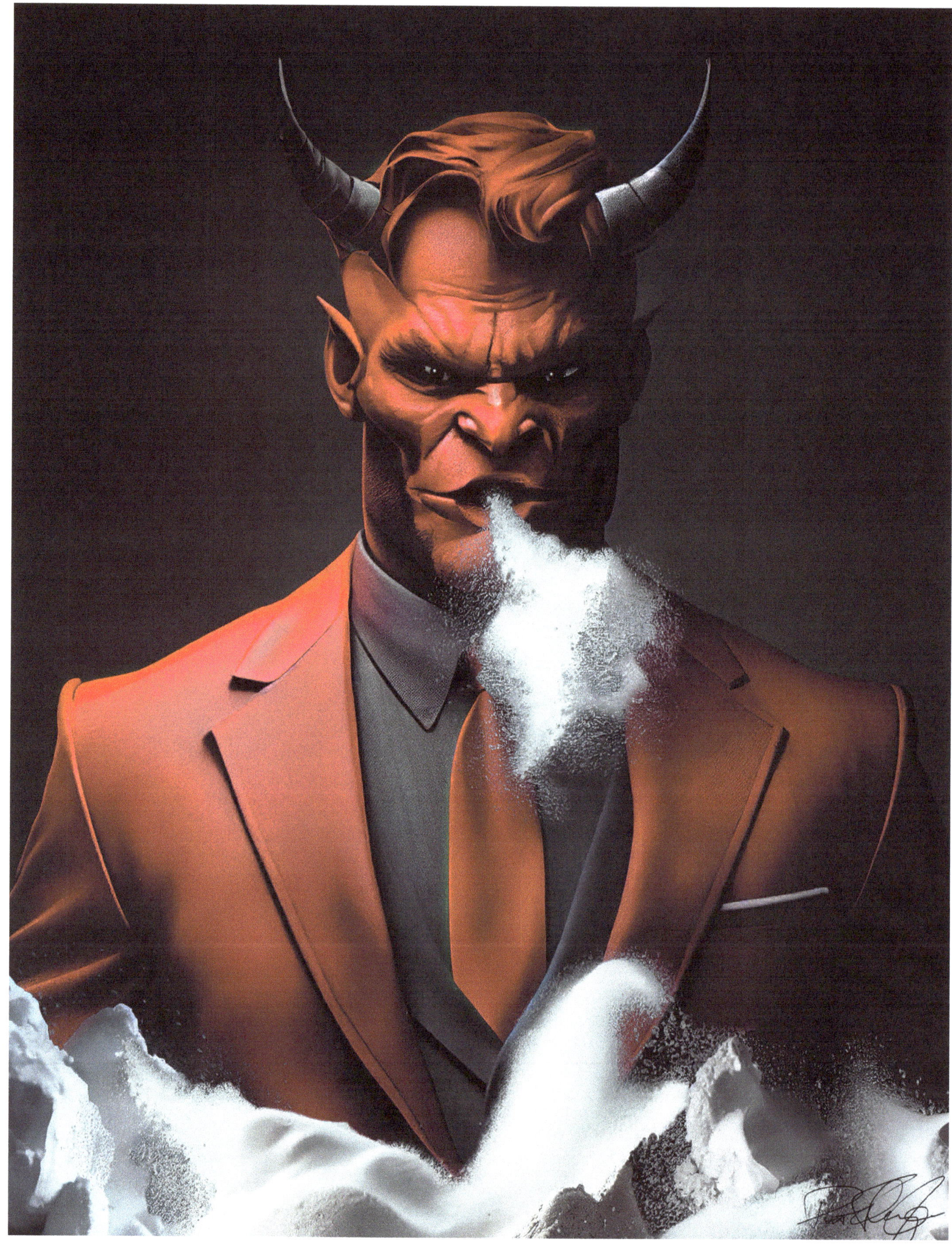

Illustration by Pat Flanagan

COCAINE

Cocaine is like the devil's kiss
It's listening to a choir of angels
All singing out of tune
It will promise you the journey of a lifetime
But you'll be riding in a rocket ship that will never reach the moon
Cocaine will mess around with your libido
Make you believe that you're some kind of superman in bed
Until you wake up the next afternoon that is
And whoever happens to be lying next to you
Will tell you that whatever you believed was going down
Was only actually going down inside your head
Cocaine has often been described as a harmless party drug
Yet it can take the strongest man down with such ease
Becoming an all-consuming need; before you realise what's happening
It becomes far more important than even the very air you actually breathe
Cocaine will turn you into Mr Popular almost overnight
No party is a party unless you're in attendance
Believe or not it will even make women find you more attractive
You can chop a line of coke out and they'll go straight down on their knees
But once the money starts to run out you'll notice an immediate difference
Starting with your special friendship with your dealer actually
Your once rock solid credit rating will disappear immediately
And you'll be subject to a form of social distancing akin to being sent to Coventry
And in desperation to maintain your habit you'll start stealing from close friends and family
And before too long they'll all begin to create distance
And unless you decide to seek help for your addiction
Before too long you'll find yourself sleeping in some doorway on the streets
Make no mistake about cocaine: it's so addictive that it doesn't take no prisoners
And it has total disregard for who it chooses to destroy
You can even go as far as saying it's the same as cancer
In that it operates a totally open and inclusive equal opportunity policy
It will happily accommodate anyone regardless of colour, race, religion, creed or gender
By simply ignoring any rules including all the so-called normal boundaries

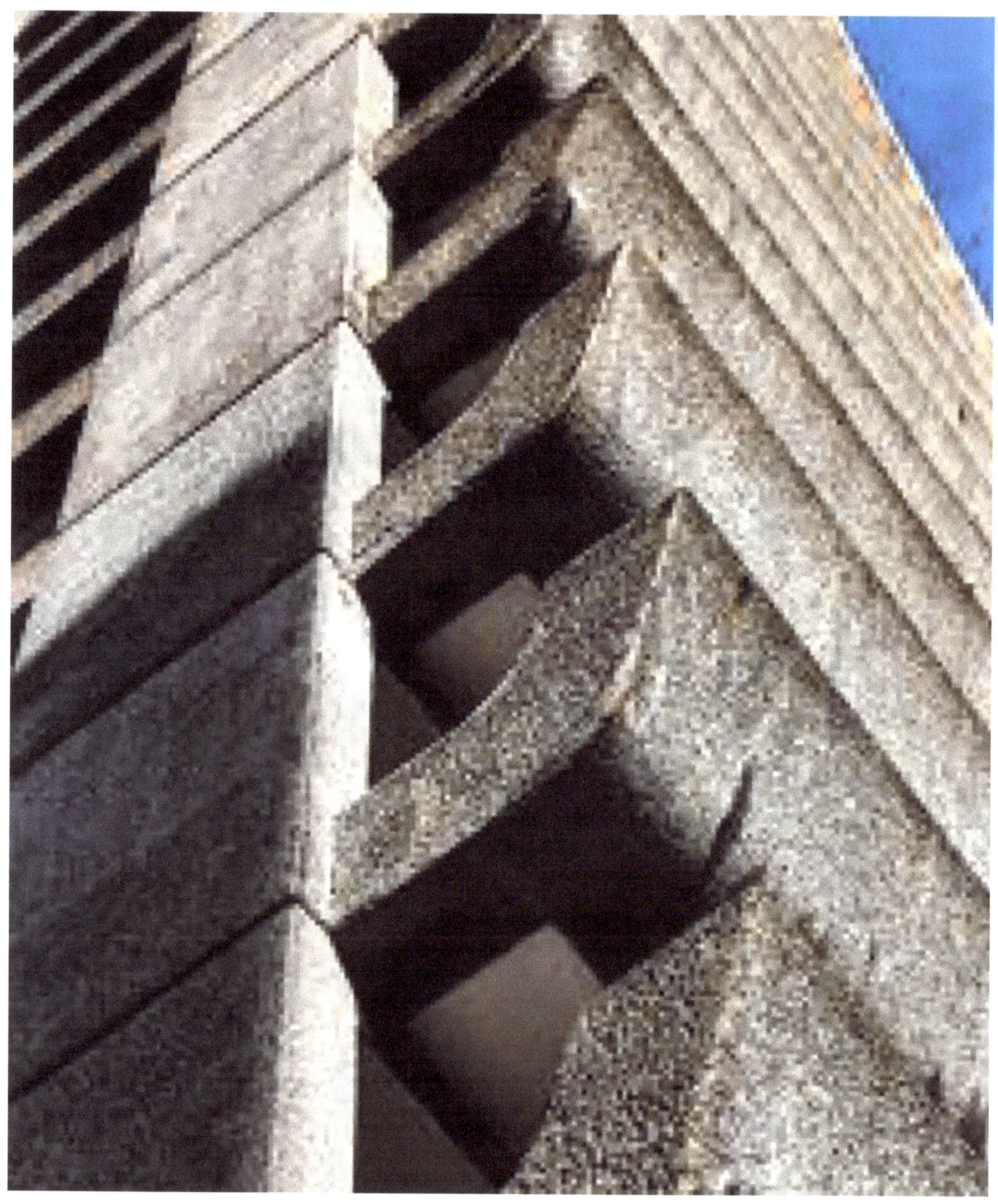

Photograph by Kevin O'Dowd

WELCOME TO MY CITY

Welcome to my city
This is where the young hearts bled
Bad boys kicking up a noise
Up inside each other's heads
A generation raised in concrete boxes
Their hopes and dreams
Frustrated and denied
Entire communities destroyed
By faceless bureaucrats
Who promised they were going
To build nirvana in the sky
But all they actually got was a front door painted sunshine yellow
And a choice of letterbox in chrome or polished brass
And as darkness falls the corridors become a no man's land
Overrun by muggers, pimps and crack addicted tarts
Old people sit and watch the world go by from their plastic windows
In total isolation inside their hermetically sealed boxes in the sky
Those days of having conversations with their next door neighbours are but now a distant memory
Those rows of little red brick houses have been replaced
By brutalist precast concrete
Towers specifically designed for modern life
With fully fitted kitchens with ergonomically designed handles
And seamless marble effect plastic worktops to add a touch of style
Inside toilet with fully fitted plastic bathroom suite and white ceramic tiles
Gas fired central heating systems to replace the old coal fires
All in all apparently a comfortable, warm, secure environment
Ideally suited to the needs of families and those who have retired
An economical construction system providing affordable social housing for the masses
And on a clear day you can even see the Woolwich ferry sail across the Thames
And if you're really lucky you might even get to see a pigeon flying by
Welcome to my part of the city
The birthplace of the brutalist movement and a fitting tribute
To those forward thinking pioneers of modular construction
Who are after all responsible for bringing grey into our lives
And lest we forget they also gave us inside toilets, central heating and electric lights
And for those of you who think that isn't such a huge achievement
You obviously haven't had to venture out in the pouring rain in winter to use an outside loo at night

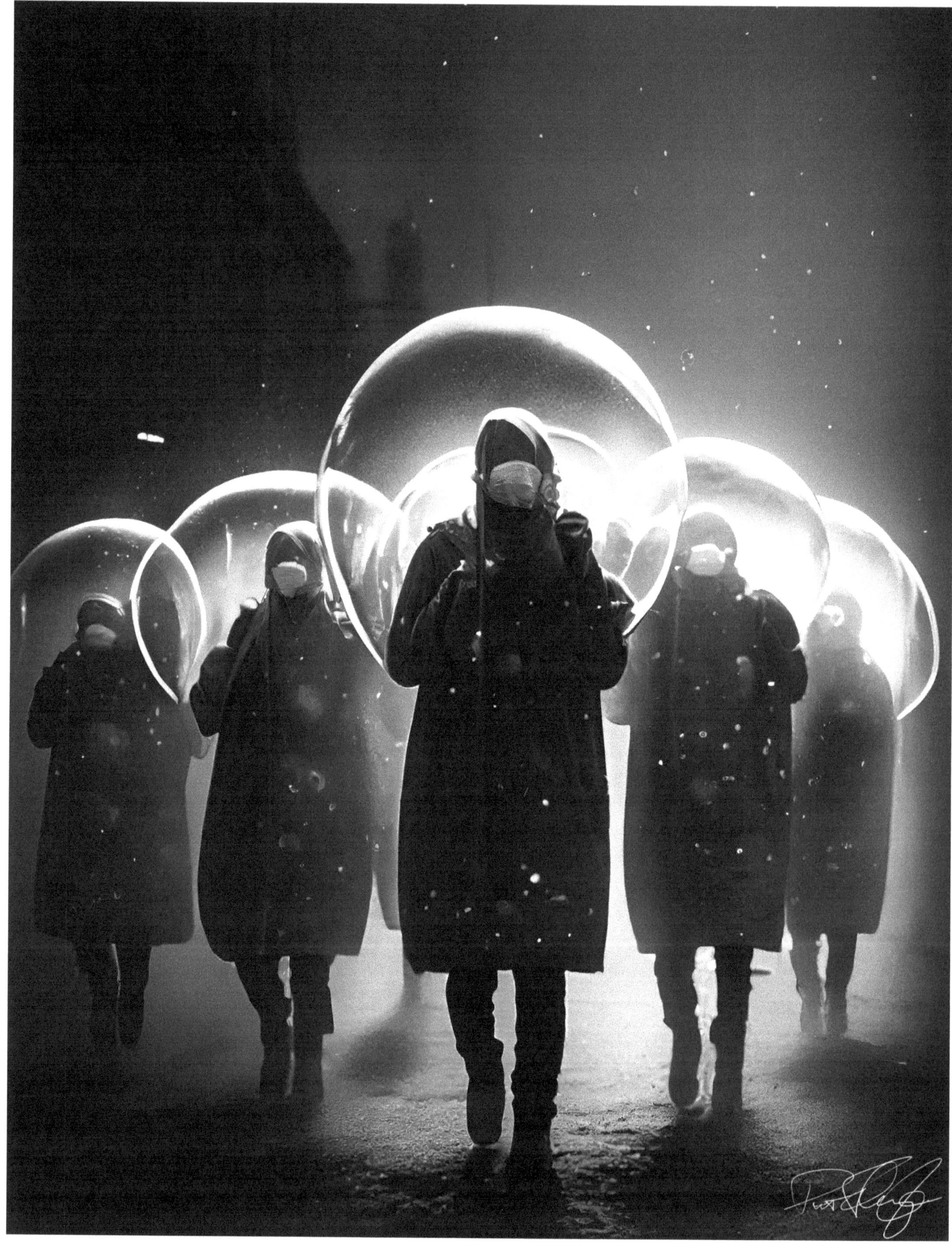

Illustration by Pat Flanagan

PANDEMIC

This tension we're feeling
Is it really there
The dark cloud of gloom
That hangs in the air
Shuffling past one another
With barely a glance
Almost as if we're afraid
To take such a chance
We've all got to stay calm
That's what we need to do
If we stick to the rules
Then life will improve
Now we're just too afraid
To make the first move
We won't enter a race
We know we can't win
We've already lost
Before we even begin
A simple decision
Becomes a mountain to climb
Not wearing a face mask
Considered a crime
Police have new powers
To issue big fines
They're clamping down hard
If we step out of line
A year spent in lockdown
Has taken its toll
On the working class people
The weak and the old
We're in this together
Well that's what they say
Apart from the politicians that is
They're still drawing full pay
People are dying
But all we can do
Is hope we don't end up
At the front of that queue
Keep two metres apart
That's what they now say
Remain in isolation
To keep each other safe

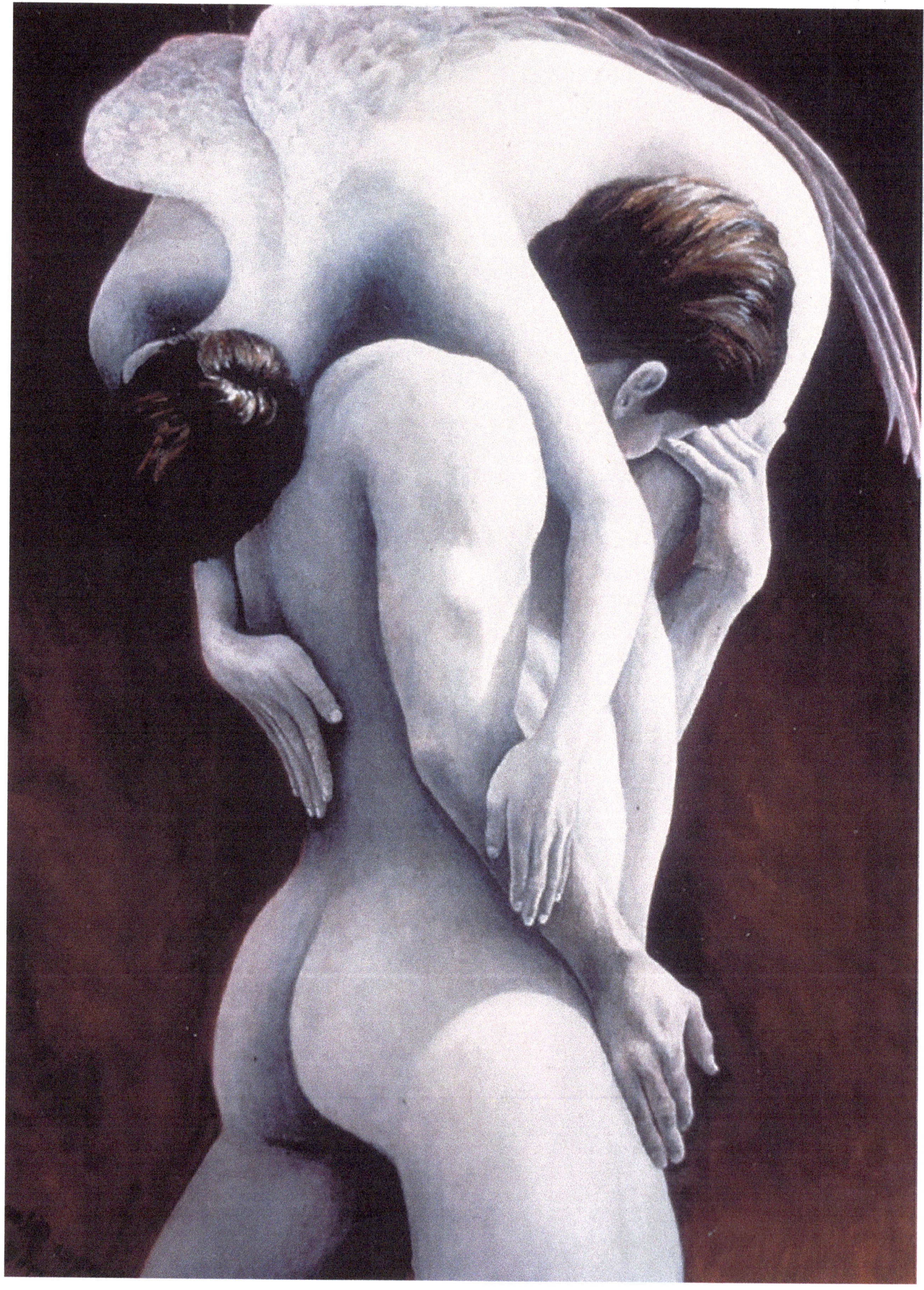

Illustration by Ginger Gilmour

I WAIT FOR SLEEP TO TAKE ME

The sky is dark
The moon has gone
The air is still
The night is long
I wait for sleep to take me
Back to where I belong
I listen to my heartbeat
The silence screams so loud
Shadows dance across the walls
As the moon escapes the clouds
Love is going to save me
I can feel it in my heart
The sun is going to shine
And lead me from the dark
Love is coming to me
I know it's on its way
I just want sleep to take me
Love will be there when I wake
I lie here listening to the clock
Tick tock tick tock tick tock
I won't know that sleep has taken me
Once the ticking stops
Love will be there in the morning
I can feel it in my heart
It will wrap its arms around me
Keep me warm when it gets dark
Love is coming back for me
We've been too long apart
I'm waiting for the morning
And a brand new start

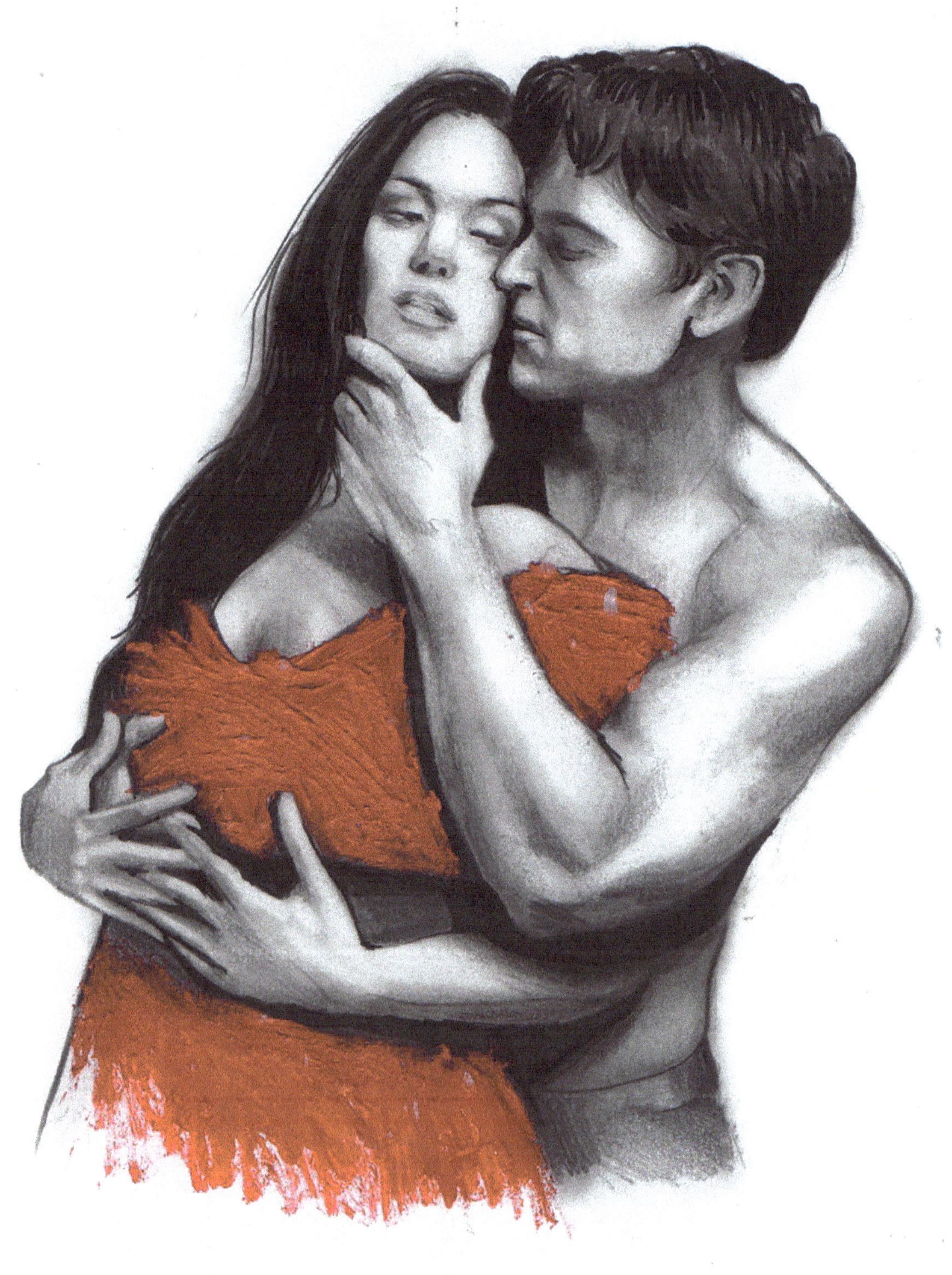

Illustration by Suzana Paula Bomfin

ONLY LOVE CAN SAVE YOU

Only love can save you
Hate will bring you down
Indecision's haunting you
In self pity you will drown
Jealousy is so destructive
It burns your bridges down
And it will leave you isolated
From those you need around
We're all in this together
We all have hopes and dreams
And not everything in life
Is quite the way it seems
Certain things go wrong
And they'll go wrong again
You're not the only one
To feel that kind of pain
It isn't always easy
To find the good in everyone
Don't try to save the world
It's a job that's never done
Don't bury disappointment
It will eat you up inside
It's always a mistake
When it's a matter of pride
Only love can save you
But you've gotta love yourself
Before putting all your energy
Into loving someone else

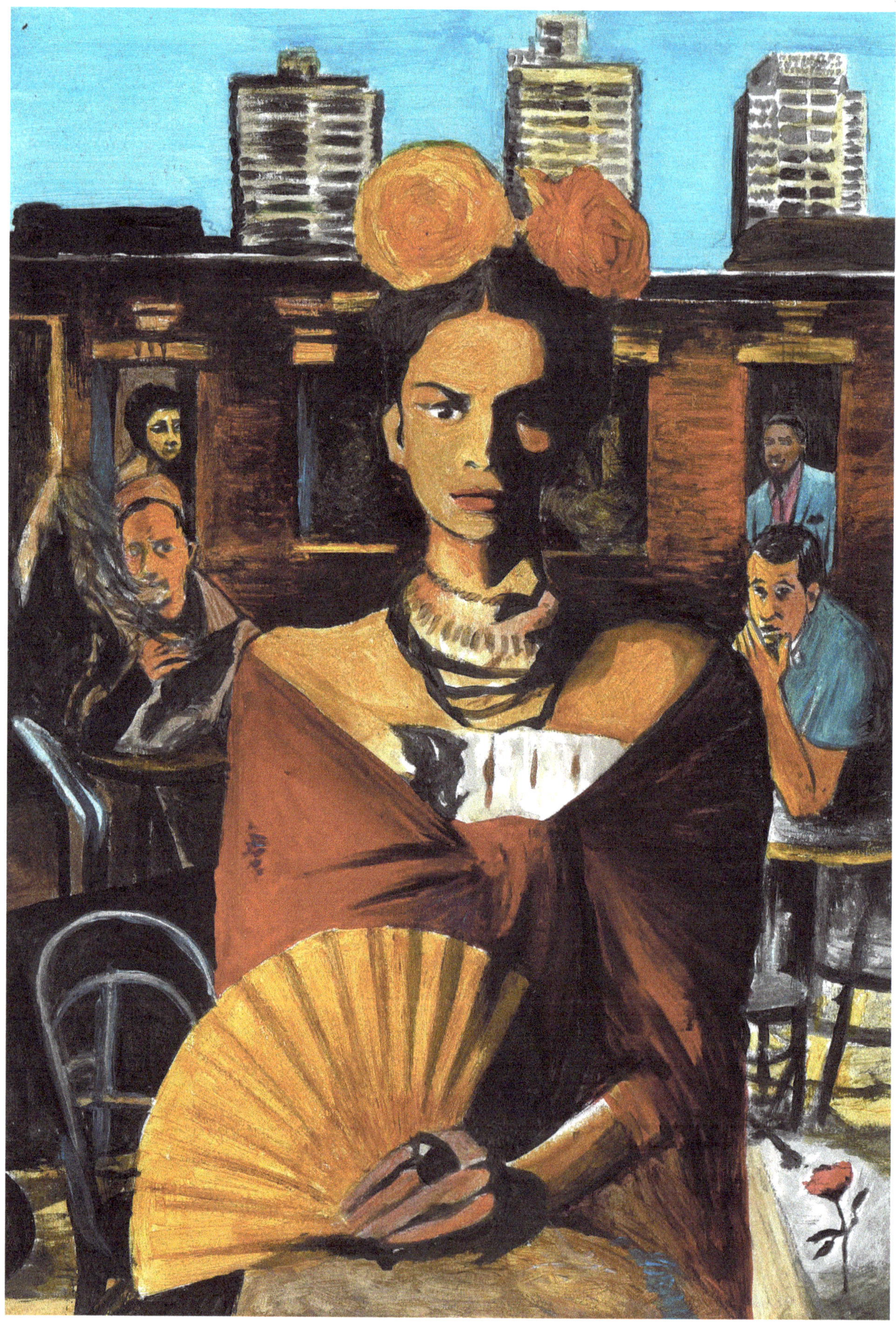

Illustration by Howard Priestley

SPANISH HARLEM

She was a million dollar baby
Born the wrong side of the street
The billboard girl with the candy bar
Stepping from a Park Lane limousine
She could stop a conversation
Make a stone heart beat
This bitch was sugar coated Hollywood
From her head down to her feet
In Spanish Harlem, Spanish Harlem
She had it all, she had it all
One of Mother Nature's finest
She weren't no fifty dollar treat
She was a New York pavement princess
A sidewalk fantasy
She had everything but nothing
Streetwise credibility
The queen without a crown
On One Hundred Twenty-Second Street
And she was bad
And I mean she was funky
Like you knew she could
And you hoped she would
In Spanish Harlem, Spanish Harlem
She had it all, she had it all
She had the body of an angel
But the devil had her mind
The kind of woman
Mothers warn their sons
Will turn a young boy blind
She would walk in smiling
With the devil by her side
Wear the kind of smug expression
That says this bitch ain't gonna hide
She'll wear her disappointment
Like some medal on her chest
Then stand real proud
And whisper loud
Honey you don't pass my test
In Spanish Harlem, she had it all

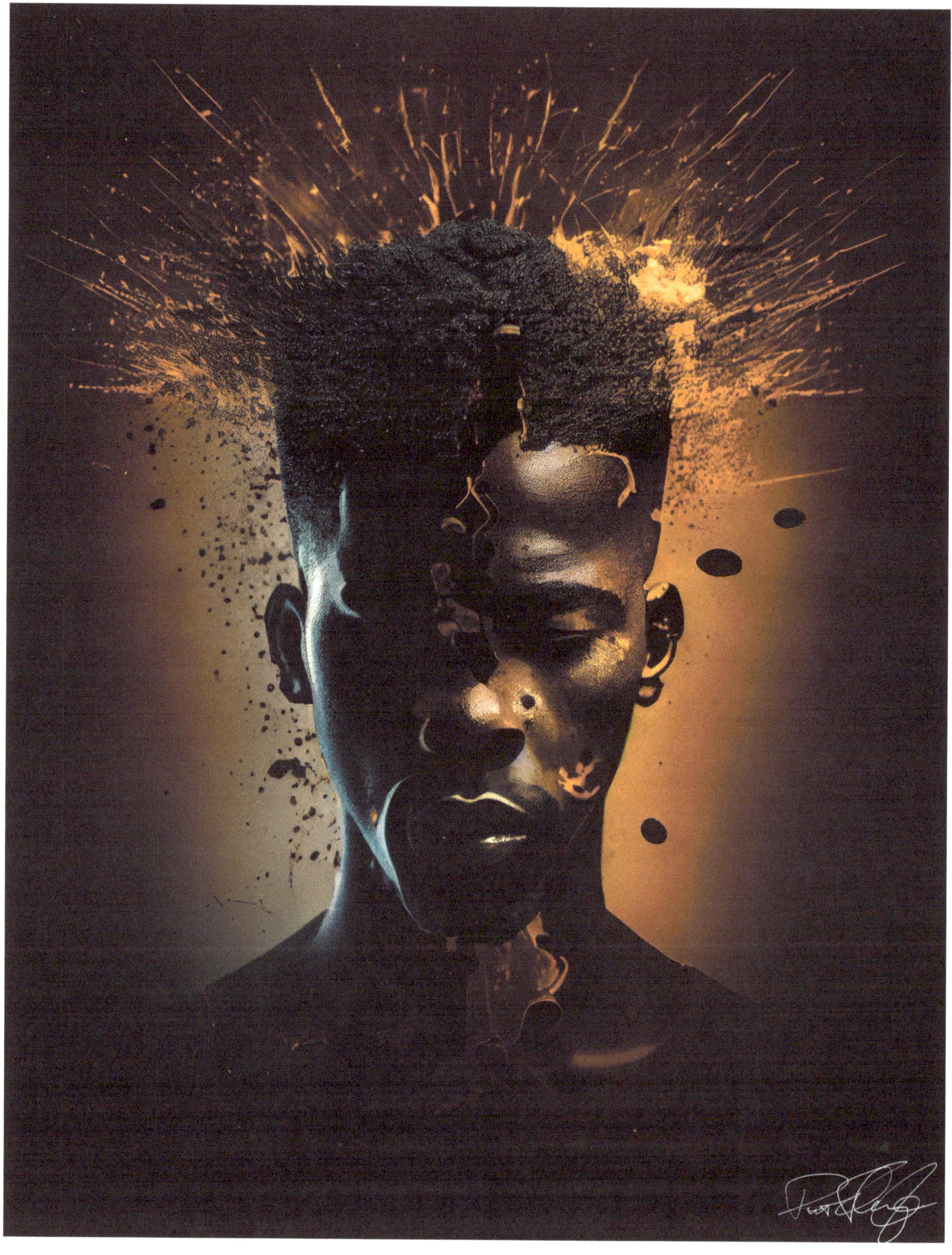

Illustration by Pat Flanagan

BOOM BOOM BANG

Another brother goes down
And turns the sidewalk red
Because a thirty-eight slug
Just slammed into his head
Boom boom bang
A boy became a man
He put his brother in a body bag
So now he gets to join the gang
Boom boom bang
The word out on the streets
Is education can't compete
Not when a fourteen-year-old home boy
Is on a grand a week
You don't need no books
To sell crack cocaine
When there's a city full of suckers
All flying on the flame
But just don't judge these brothers
Because you've misunderstood
He may well be a sucker
But this sucker's
Running with the hood
Boom boom bang

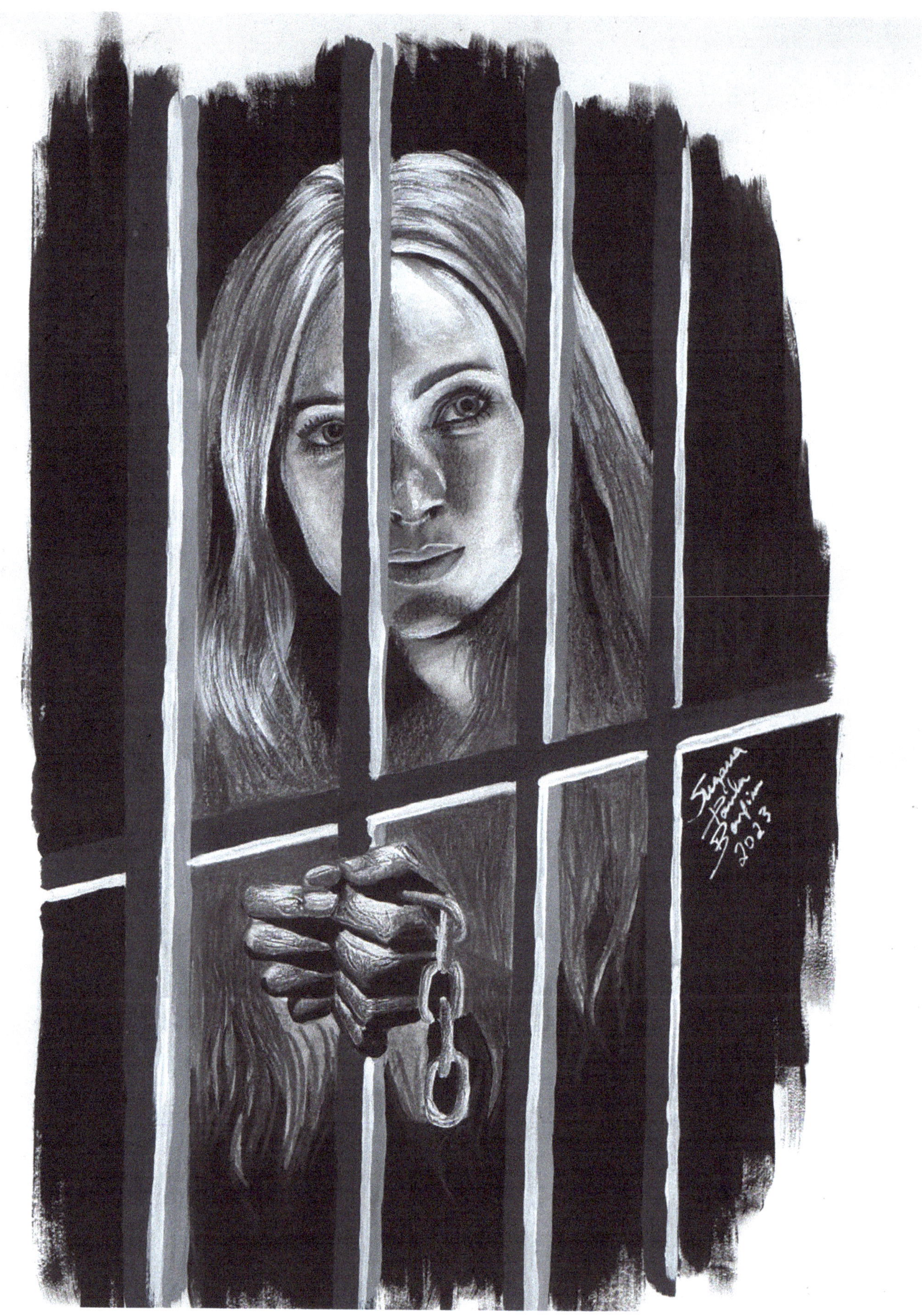

Illustration by Suzana Paula Bomfin

THAT'S WHAT LOVE'S ABOUT

In so many different ways
For some it will be flowers
For others simply praise
Some will shower you with gifts
Whilst others use kind words
Some will choose to set you free
Others cage you like a bird
Some will give their lives for you
Some will even share your pain
Be there to pick you up
Each time it rains on your parade
Some will promise you the world
Along with everything within it
They'll always be there at your side
With a loyalty beyond all normal limits
Some will fill your heart with joy
Others cripple you with pain
Some will walk into your life
Then simply disappear again
Some will make you very happy
Some will make you sad
They will leave you feeling incomplete
And even drive you fucking mad
But then that's what love is all about
Just like the tide that ebbs and flows
You'll hardly ever see it coming
But you'll always notice when it goes

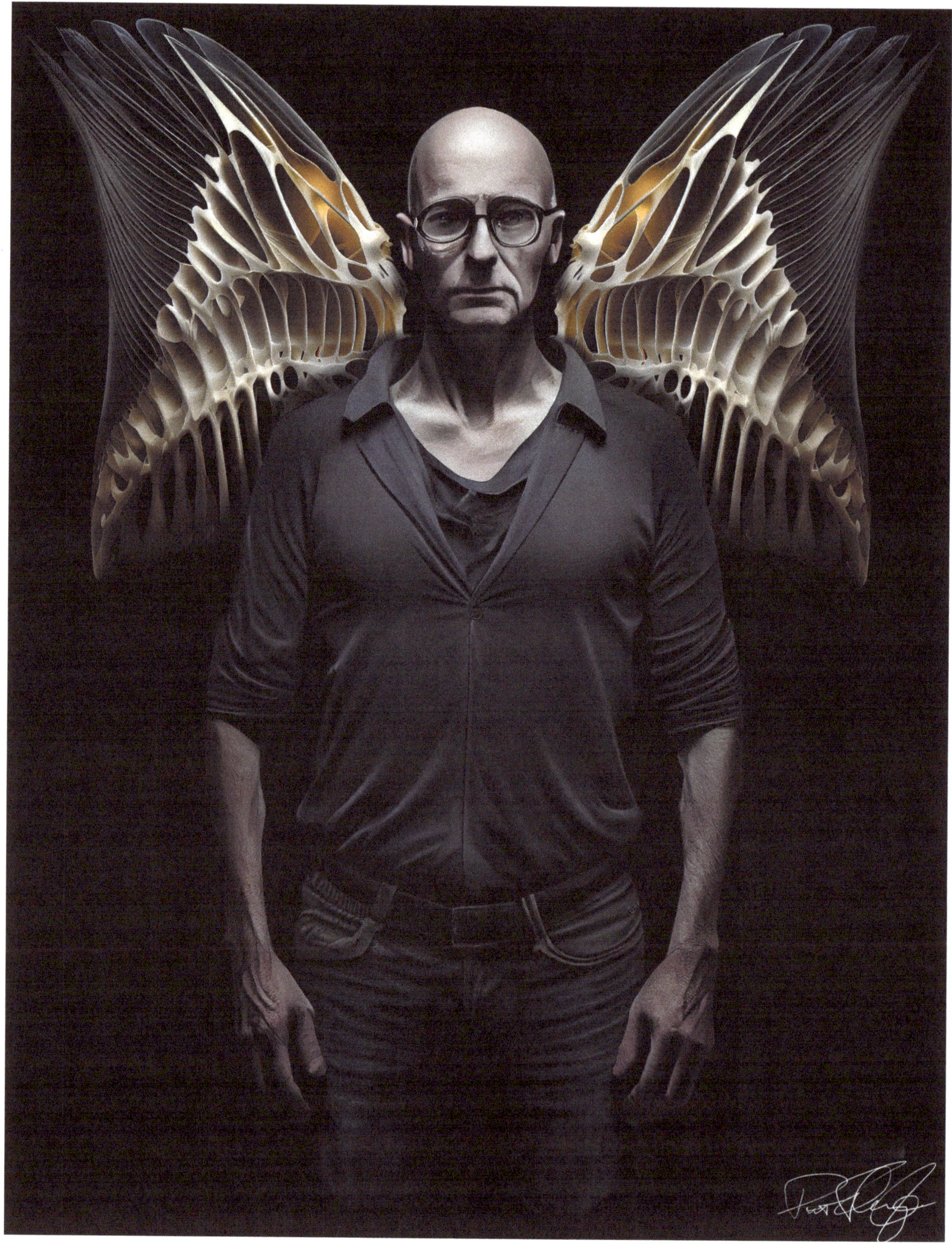

Illustration by Pat Flanagan

AIN'T NO ANGEL

I ain't no angel
With torn and battered wings
No streetwise hippie homeboy
Trying to spread myself too thin
My mother ain't no duchess
And my old man ain't no king
So if there's any blue blood
In my veins
You won't see it through my skin
I ain't no refugee from Harlem
Hanging high on crack
Some disappointed Dylan freak
Seeking solitude through smack
I've never screamed in silence
The world can hear what's in my head
And I don't remember ever telling you
That you would have to share my bed

MEET THE ARTISTS

Boy George needs no introduction. Since bursting on to the music scene in the 1980s, he has continued to be culturally significant, not just in the UK, but worldwide. Be it through his music, his fashion, his art, or just his opinions, he has continued to make headlines.
His art business continues to go from strength to strength, from his first solo exhibition in Monte Carlo in 2019, to his sell out show in Copenhagen in 2022. After the initial exhibition sold out, demand was so high for his work that his entire private collection, hanging in his Hampstead home, was purchased by the gallery to be sold on to collectors.
George's original canvasses, which are a combination of paint, beads and sequins, (all individually sewn on), his silk screen prints and his NFTs, all showcase his unique and very recognisable style. Although very different media types, they all work beautifully side by side, as a complete collection. **Instagram** @boygeorgeofficial

******

Suzi Quatro needs no introduction either. Her long career as a rock icon, actress and author spans several decades and she is still touring and making new music. She is one of the most prolific rock and roll stars of the last half century. **www.suziquatro.com**

******

Mark Wardel AKA TradeMark is a contemporary artist whose work explores issues of identity, portraiture and the self created personae prevalent within the entertainment industry, club and urban LGBT+ sub cultures. His distinctive hand painted work draws on influences from traditional portraiture through post punk graphics, New York urban art of the 70s/80s, Soviet era propaganda posters,1950s male physique photos, pop art and contemporary high-fashion imagery and has been exhibited in galleries and museums internationally, including London's V&A museum for whom he created an edition of 300 David Bowie life mask sculptures as part of their record breaking 'David Bowie Is' exhibition in 2013. Clients include… Soho House Films, Absolute Vodka, David Bowie/Isolar New York, Homotopia Festival, Dazed and Confused, Boy George, EMI Records, Defected Records. Mark Wardel lives and works in London.
Website markwardel.com **Online store** trashDNA.com **Instagram** mark_wardel **Twitter**@TradeMarkArt

******

Ginger Gilmour is an accomplished artist and has had several exhibitions in the UK and USA. She paints and sculpts and her work is that of seeking beauty and peace. Ginger came to the UK many years ago from the US, as musician (Pink Floyd) David Gilmour's first wife. She made the UK her home for her and her 4 wonderful children.

You can contact Ginger at
www.gingergilmour.co.uk
Ginger is soon releasing her autobiography, also published by New Haven Publishing Ltd

******

Dean Stockings is primarily a photographer and videographer, although he also creates graphic illustrations. Shooting for magazines as far afield as Australia, Europe and the USA, his work has graced the covers of many international publications (over 300 to date) and been included in exhibitions and photographic anthologies around the world. There have been various interviews and articles in the press, including the prestigious international photography magazine ZOOM, (Italy), The Independent newspaper (UK), and Professional Photographer Magazine (UK), which ran a six page feature on him entitled *A Day in the Life of Dean Stockings.*
He has worked on video content for Billboard and Sky Arts amongst others. He currently works as Boy George's Head of Art. **Instagram** @deanstockings

******

Simon Thompson has a lifelong passion for art, illustration and design. After finishing Art School, he established his career as a designer, art director and illustrator.
After having a stroke in 2018, his artistic work took on a new lease of life and he continues to design books and magazines, while also pursuing his passion of portrait painting and illustration. He loves film, music and art and draws inspiration from artists including Bisley, Franzetta and Sienkiewicz. Simon lives in North West London. He has two daughters, Rose and Hannah, and Walnut the cat. **www.alteredimagesdesign.com**

******

Pat Flanagan "Disruption. I believe art should disrupt, disturb, evoke, provoke, and even polarize." I am a digital artist who lives in Seattle. I've been active in digital art since the mid 1980s, starting with mathematical art, then moving to freehand digital creations, all self-taught. Born in 1967, I grew up through the musical revolutions of punk, electronic music, and new wave. Each disruptive of the prior, each a rejection of the past. The music I grew up with shaped my artistic viewpoint. While I'm primarily interested in blending real and surreal, I also enjoy the challenge of exploring varying styles. Until now, my art has been for my own enjoyment, as well as occasional commercial graphic design for clients. Kevin's book contains my first officially published pieces. My work can be viewed and acquired at **www.PatFlanagan.com**

******

Albert Laslo Haines who creates, from imagination, one off works, sometimes intricate, detailed and vibrant, other times dark and moody.

******

Suzana Paula Bomfin
Journalist, polyglot, sculptor, painter and illustrator born in Rio de Janeiro, Brazil. Working with fine art and commissioned portraits worldwide, known mostly for ambidextrous art works and different techniques and realistic details. Influenced by renaissance artists such as DaVinci, she also uses her artistic skills for vegan activism. **Suzannab6@hotmail.com**
Instagram: @suz.art

******

Russ Leach is an award winning *Batman* and *Dr Who* artist with a career in production spanning nearly 40 years. In that time he has accrued a long list of credits producing design, tech and publishing projects for a wide variety of clients including DC, BBC, Marvel, Cartoon Network, Panini, Markosia, Wizard and Sony to name just a few. Since 2010, Russ has immersed himself in his first love of sequential art, working on various periodical publications (Hero Time presents Batman, Dr Who Magazine, Ben 10 Magazine, Dr Who Adventures, Draw The Marvel Way) as well as multiple graphic novels (Only Death Can Save Us volume 1 and 2, The Indifference Engine 2 and Terminus at Fenton's Green). With a healthy mix of mainstream and indie publications to his name as well as story boarding for both tech and film, Russ is involved in a constant stream of projects working with top publishers and talent.
Website: www.russleach.com
email : art_info@kre8uk.net

******

Howard Priestley was born in Halifax, West Yorkshire in 1956. He has always had an equal interest in African-American culture and comic books. At the same time as he began his formal Art studies at Stourbridge in the West Midlands he became a regular contributor to the British Comics Fan scene and on completing his Fine Art Degree, where he wrote his thesis on Holland Dozier Holland, he returned home and published a 3 issue series, Shock Therapy. The work from this period was credited in the book, Nasty Tales – A History Of The British Underground Comic Scene, 2000. He has designed CD cover art for Bootsy Collins, George Clinton and Jerome Brailey as well as writing histories for several CD compilations. He helped to develop community radio in Calderdale, Phoenix FM and hosts The Soul City Show which has included interviews with Eddie Holland, Marvin Junior of The Dells, Melvin Davis and Richard Street of The Temptations. As a writer he has contributed to magazines such as Blues & Soul, Soul Express and MOJO magazine as well as writing a regular column on Funk for the fanzine Soul Up North. Priestley won the 2022 Winner of the Award for Excellence in Historical Recorded Sound Research - Association of Recorded Sound Collections ARSO for his book *Love Factory: The History of Holland Dozier Holland*
Website: www.howardpriestley.co.uk

******

Julie Bennett London-based artist Julie Bennett specialises in portraiture. Her bold, unapologetically confident portraits have an overly-exaggerated painted surface as a juxtaposition to our digital world. She was listed as one of the Top 20 artists to own in 2022 by London-based gallery DegreeArt, who showcased her work at the Affordable Art Fair following a successful six-week artist residency at the five-star art hotel Bankside Hotel, London. Bennett has widely exhibited in group exhibitions, which include Mall Galleries, V&A Museum, and Saatchi Online, among others. Her work has been published in Stylist, Classic Rock, The Sunday Times, Independent, and The Guardian. Bennett made six short films on painting for BBC Bitesize. Bennett's works are held in a number of private collections in the UK and internationally.
Website: www.juliebennett.co.uk

******

Dusty O is a London based contemporary artist, writer and activist. Dusty was a well known drag performer and club promoter before their art career began 7 years ago. Dusty has held 6 solo exhibitions and was the first LGBTQ artist to be invited to show at The Houses of Parliament. They are currently preparing for a show at Brain Brunn Gallery in Tokyo in September. Dusty has written a best selling memoire called *"The Boy Who Sat By The Window"* under their birth name of David Hodge. Their art can be seen at **@artbydustyo** on Instagram

******

Shaun George I'm 55 and I self taught myself to draw during my recovery from cancer in 2014, I needed a distraction from the effects of chemo and radio treatment. Over the years I have fine tuned my drawing style from detailed mandala art to abstract pop art, and more lately moving onto digital art. I am also keen on photography and also dabble in astro-photography.
I can be found on instagram under the name **astro_and_artmk** where you can view my work.
Please feel free to drop me a message.
My email is **shauninuk@hotmail.com**

******

Gerald O'Dowd is an artist/photographer/film maker/poet and lyricist who works in several different mediums including making short films for community based projects and doing voluntary work with people with disabilities and mental health issues and he is also my fabulous brother. Email:
Gerald411@btinternet.com

www.ingramcontent.com/pod-product-compliance
Lightning Source LLC
LaVergne TN
LVHW070459120826
845154LV00019BA/95

9781912587834